THE GEORGE CARLIN LETTERS

THE PERMANENT COURTSHIP OF SALLY WADE

Sally WADE

THE GEORGE CARLIN LETTERS

THE PERMANENT COURTSHIP OF SALLY WADE

Sally WADE

G

GALLERY BOOKS

NEW YORK   LONDON   TORONTO   SYDNEY

THERE'S NO BETTER
PLACE IN THE WORLD
THAN THE ~~XXXX~~ ROOM
WHERE SALLY WADE IS
LOCATED.

— G. CARLIN

"**Just remember these words in my story—cutie pie, thoughtful, considerate, loving, warm—just pile it on, baby—after that, you can say anything you want.**"

So here goes . . .

Gallery Books
A Division of Simon & Schuster, Inc.
1230 Avenue of the Americas
New York, NY 10020

First Gallery Books hardcover edition March 2011

GALLERY BOOKS and colophon are trademarks of Simon & Schuster, Inc.

For information about special discounts for bulk purchases, please contact Simon & Schuster Special Sales at 1-866-506-1949 or business@simonandschuster.com

The Simon & Schuster Speakers Bureau can bring authors to your live event. For more information or to book an event contact the Simon & Schuster Speakers Bureau at 1-866-248-3049 or visit our website at www.simonspeakers.com.

Designed by Jane Archer /www.psbella.com

Manufactured in the United States of America

10 9 8 7 6 5 4 3 2 1

Library of Congress Cataloging-in-Publication Data

Wade, Sally.
    The George Carlin letters : the permanent courtship of Sally Wade / Sally Wade. — 1st Gallery Books hardcover ed.
        p. cm.
    1. Carlin, George. 2. Comedians—United States—Biography. 3. Wade, Sally. 4. Screenwriters—United States—Biography. I. Title.
    PN2287.C2685W34 2011
    792.7′6028092—dc22
    [B]   2010045525

ISBN 978-1-4516-0776-5
ISBN 978-1-4516-1140-3 (ebook)

contents

The day Geo died, I came home and found this note propped up in front of my computer screen. George had left it for me before he went to the hospital.

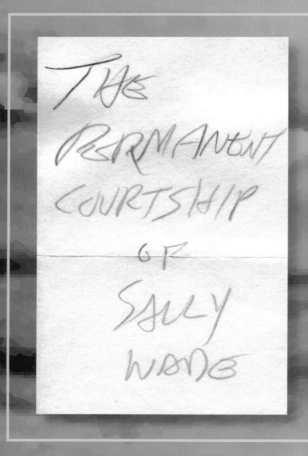

THE

PERMANENT

COURTSHIP

OF

SALLY

WADE

The instant I saw the note, even through my devastation, I knew—as he did—that this is the book I was meant to write. A book about our love story.

My dog **Spot** disagreed at first— he felt his book should come first—the one I was working on with Geo: I was Spot's channeler and scribe; Geo was his editor, agent, personal assistant, personal chef, and drug supplier for extra hip dysplasia meds. But when I showed Spot Geo's note, he agreed that his own book would have to wait—and to my amazement, even agreed to pitch in!

Feeling more and more like my idol, *Ruth Gordon*, with Spot as my sidekick Clyde, the orangutan from *Every Which Way But Loose,* I somehow managed to keep things organized enough to put this book together—another one for the annals of **Jupiter.** Which is where we believe we're from and where we'll end up someday . . .

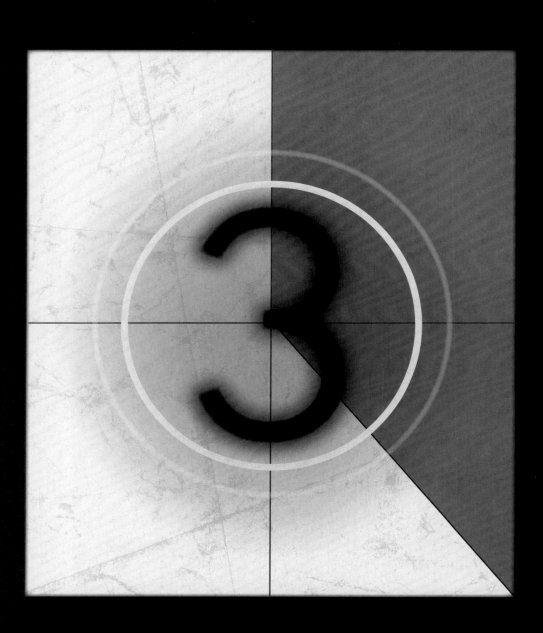

CANAL PRODUCTIONS

PRESENTS

A SALLY WADE FILM

- GEORGE CARLIN -

SALLY and WADE

IN

" THE JUPITERIANS "

FEATURING SPOT THE WONDER DOG

Hey Hollywood Dialie —

(FADE IN)

—INT. BOOKSTORE - DAY—

AN ATTRACTIVE WOMAN WITH A
BLOND COCKER SPANIEL IS EYEING
A GOOD-LOOKING MALE CUSTOMER
WAITING AT THE COUNTER. SHE IS
INTERESTED. THE DOG PICKS UP HER
VIBE AND AMBLES OVER TO THE MALE
CUSTOMER TO MAKE FRIENDS ON BE-
HALF OF HIS MISTRESS. THE MAN
IS FRIENDLY AND WARM TOWARD THE
DOG — IMPRESSING THE WOMAN AND MAK-
ING THE MAN EVEN MORE ATTRACTIVE
TO HER. WITHIN ONE YEAR SHE WAS
STRADDLING HIM + SHOWING HIM HER TITS.

CHAPTER 1

A Cute Meet

AN ATTRACTIVE WOMAN (*played by me, Sally Wade*) WITH A BLOND COCKER SPANIEL (*otherwise known as Spot, my dog*) IS EYEING A GOOD-LOOKING MALE CUSTOMER WAITING AT THE COUNTER. THEY ARE IN A BOOKSTORE IN SANTA MONICA, CALIFORNIA, CALLED DUTTON'S.

I hear his voice before I turn and see him, standing at the counter—it's unmistakable and raspy: "I'll take *Our Culture and What's Left of It, The Anatomy of Dirty Words,* and *Rationale of the Dirty Joke* . . . and if ya can get 'em to me by Friday," he says to the clerk who's helping him, "I'll give ya a tip to buy yourself some weed."

My hair is tucked up under a hat, I have sunglasses on, and I'm wearing the same baggy-ass sweatsuit I slept in the night before. He is wearing baggy sweatpants, a T-shirt, and a hat. In other words, we match. In fact, we look like one of those couples who have decided to dress alike.

THE DOG (*Spot*) PICKS UP HER VIBE AND AMBLES OVER TO THE GOOD-LOOKING MALE CUSTOMER (*Geo*) TO MAKE FRIENDS ON BEHALF OF HIS MISTRESS (*Sal*).

Geo is friendly and warm to Spot. In fact, what I didn't know then, is that they already knew each other. They used to hustle on the streets of Kansas City, Missouri, until Spot was "pinched" and Geo got "shot," back in the early nineties.

YEAH, I KNEW SPOT BACK IN K.C.

ABOUT 6 YEARS AGO. HE WAS HEAVY.

A card from Geo, reminiscing about his early hustling days with Spot

NOTE FROM GEO: Dog depicted here is fictitious. Any similarity to the actual dog is just out of the question.

I RAN WITH SPOT FOR ABOUT 6 MONTHS DURIN' THE EARLY 90'S. WE WERE RUNNIN' STREET HUSTLES AND "LOST-DOG" SCAMS ON THE WEST SIDE TILL SPOT GOT PINCHED AND SENT AWAY FOR 2 to 5. I GOT SHOT THE FOLLOWIN' WEEK AND HAD TO QUIT THE GAME. I STILL MISS THE STREET AND THE HUSTLE AND I REALLY MISS RUNNIN' WITH SPOT. TELL HIM TO HANG IN AND KEEP LICKIN' HIS PAWS.

Sal wants to introduce herself, but needs a sign from the universe—and nothing short of him saying "hello" to her first will work. Spot, always one step ahead, beats her to it and walks right over to him: "Sally, George—George, Sally . . ."

NOTE FROM SAL: A young Spot, "pinched and sent away for 2 to 5"

"Sally, George—

George, Sally . . .

Sal, Geo—Geo, Sal."

"She's a comedy writer who has written for TV and movies, and he's a comedic genius who's published his first book, *Brain Droppings*."

Then George invites Sally to see his show in Vegas, and say "hello" backstage. There it is—"hello"—Sally's sign from the universe.

If I knew what was going to happen next . . .

"WITHIN ONE YEAR SHE WAS STRADDLING HIM AND SHOWING HIM HER TITS . . ."

I'm not sure if I should give credit to Spot or destiny. And like Dorothy said to her dog, Toto, in another fantasy . . .

"I guess we're not in Kansas anymore . . ."

Only this time, it's my dog saying it to me.

This is what's called a
"cute meet"
in the movies.

Hey, Sister —
See THAT TWISTER? THAT'S WHAT
YOU DID TO MY HEART — STIRRED
EVERYTHING UP AND CHANGED MY
WHOLE INNER GEOGRAPHY.
    WE'RE NOT IN KANSAS ANYMORE,
COOKIE — WE'RE IN LOVE!!

    YOU THE BEST,
        YOU MY SWEET GIRL,
            YOU THE SUN & THE
                MOON AND THE
        QUEEN OF JUPITER!
            I LOVE YOU, SIS. MORE

In Vegas, at Bally's, in Wayne Newton's old theater, is the *George Carlin Show*. I watch George's act, but I don't remember much about it, because **I'm preoccupied and thinking about something else . . .**

HIM. ➡

And whether or not he'll recognize me without a hat on. I'm wearing a new brown Jil Sander suit from Barney's. **That's right, I bought a suit to wear on my first date.** With GEORGE CARLIN. And a white button-down shirt, that has two buttons near the collar, so it'll stay put. I thought he'd appreciate the fine craftsmanship . . .

HI BABE!

HEY GOOFY — WHERE THE FUCK ARE YOU? GET DOWN HERE!! I MISS YOU.

BEIN' WITHOUT YOU IS LIKE HAVING NO AIR, SUNLIGHT, SCENERY, STARS, CLOUDS, BIRDS, FLOWERS OR TREES.

I, of course, recognize him right away—he's the one onstage with the microphone in his hand, shouting

"FUCK YOU!"

at the crowd. *Figuring that out is half the battle,* I think, trying to convince myself that the glass is "half full." Or is it the bottle? I ask myself, nervously eying my wine glass, which was getting low.

After the show, I go backstage. How'd I get backstage? I walked. I unhooked Spot's leash at the back entrance, then together we walked down the outer aisle, through a door behind the curtain, past topless, half-naked women from the show before his in the hallway (where I realize they share the same dressing room), and nobody stopped me. Either security was lax that day—this was before 9/11—or Spot and I just looked like we belonged.

Backstage, in the dressing room, sitting on a bar stool, is the handsome, charming, and friendly George Carlin, sipping a Diet Coke. When I enter the room, he looks up at me and says,

"Hey, there's Spot's Mom!"

I'm your ever-lovin' baby.

YOU FILL MY HEART WITH BIG, BURSTING PINWHEELS OF SPARKLING JOY.

MAN, I CAN'T WAIT TO SEE YOUR FACE.

Spot shakes Geo's hand and says, "What are ya, one of those Rain Man–type of guys who can keep everything in their head? You didn't miss a line! At least not one of mine!" he tells Geo, establishing his dominance right away.

Through a long, mostly vacant corridor, toward the back entrance, Geo walks me to my car. Right away we're having a good conversation. I can tell because he says,

"I think I'm losing my sense of smell because I can't tell if I fart anymore."

I say, "Well, if everybody starts waving their arms in the air or opening windows and jumping, there's your clue . . ."

"Ya into gamblin'?" Geo asks Sal.

"Yeah, In fact, last night, I got up eight million dollars at the Frontier, then went across the street to the Mirage and lost it all in the quarter machine."

Geo offers to call "Vegas Problem Solvers," to see if they can fix the problem, but Spot says he already has. "I'm way ahead of ya on that one, budd!"

When a valet brings my car around to the back entrance, Geo tells me he'll call me in four months—and that, "We'll go have a bagel after that." Which I find out later is the same length of time it will take for him to fulfill a year of mourning since his wife passed away. *Because that's just the kind of guy he is—the "stand-up" kind.* But at the time I wonder if I'll ever see him again.

On the car ride home, I say to Spot, "Who says, 'I'll call ya in four months and we'll go have a bagel'?"

> " I'll call ya in four months and we'll go have a bagel. "

"George Carlin," Spot says. "He just did. Didn't you hear him?"

Four months is an awfully long time to wait for a bagel, I'm thinking. But fortunately, the drive back to L.A. is peaceful, and I'm able to clear my head. In fact, I learn something new—which is that driving long distances like that, across a wide expanse of desert . . .with all that quiet time to let your soul speak to your spirit—I realize that things like "getting ahead," "inner drive," and "ambition" are just a big diversion from loafing.

Or else I'm in love . . .

Greetings from Las Vegas

POST CARD

MS. SALLY WADE

SIS! THE NEXT YEAR, YOU WERE BORN, AND THE WORLD BEGAN. SIX MONTHS LATER I JOINED THE AIR FORCE AND BEGAN MY JOURNEY TOWARD YOU. TOOK A WHILE, BUT HERE WE ARE. HERE I AM. COLLISION SHIT! JUST LIKE THAT "STRING-OF-PEARLS" COMET THAT HIT JUPITER. POW! POW! POW! POW! POW! POW! A GOOD RHYTHM - JUST LIKE OURS. TWO HEARTBEATS IN RHYME. SENDING YOU GREAT SPARKS. I AM GEORGE, AND YOURS!

Geo looking over the fence, checking out Sal's new sod.

CHAPTER 2

Four Months Later

He calls. But before that, while I'm waiting for his call, I try to fix up my house on the canals in Venice, California. Outside, I even put new sod in the yard so he won't know Spot is a digger.

Then I work on the interior of the house, beginning with the dirty dishes. Some dishes aren't clean enough to put in the dishwasher, so I end up throwing them away. Other junk, I throw out the window of my car—like old CDs and stuff. Littering . . . it's my last guilty pleasure.

Once I threw an ugly old sofa off the second-story balcony of my ex-husband's house in Kansas. His mother never did like me after that. (My mother-in-law did teach me how to get rid of the hiccups though, so I really can't complain.) Which reminds me, before Geo calls to go get a bagel . . . I get a divorce. Hiccup! That way Geo won't be dating a married woman. All that was left to finalize it was to have the divorce papers notarized.

I went to Mail Boxes, Etc. on Twenty-sixth and San Vicente in Santa Monica, because they've got a notary there—plus, they sell boxes. So you can sign on the dotted line and pack up all your shit at the same time. Kill two birds with one stone, that way. By the way, they've since changed the name to "Postal & More." Now you know why.

My estranged spouse and I were already separated and living apart. I call him my *estranged spouse,* not because we weren't divorced, but because if you take the first and last letter off the word **"e-strange-d,"** you get a better picture of him. I met him in college, at the University of Kansas, and my understanding was that he would move out here to California at some future date. I guess I should have asked. I think I did. But in fairness to both parties, I could've heard wrong.

As it turns out, I never could get him to sell the family farm. Which is considered a sin in the Midwest, by the way—akin to murder, although closer to treason. Because where your cow wants to live is far more important than where your wife does.

Spot tells people he *was* the divorce settlement, although he doesn't hold a grudge. He also wants me to point out that it took three coon dogs, all singing in unison with a pack of howling coyotes, for my estranged spouse to replace him. That's how invaluable he was in the mediation process.

   "So it took three dogs to replace just this one dog?" Geo asked when I told him. "No wonder he's got problems."

The mayor of Buck Creek

David McEnery
Mud Dreams

HEY CUTIE —
THE MAYOR OF BUCK CREEK SLEEPS OFF A DRUNKEN SPREE AND DREAMS OF RUNNING FOR PRESIDENT, WITH SPOT AS HIS RUNNING MATE. UNBEKNOWNST TO HIM, SPOT IS PLANNING TO RUN FOR THE TOP SPOT ON HIS OWN, WITH THE SLOGAN "VOTE FOR ME, AND I WILL SHIT IN YOUR NEIGHBOR'S DOORWAY." INSIDERS SAY GORE AND BUSH ARE THREATENING TO REVEAL SPOT'S PAST AS A CAT FUCKER. STAY TUNED

GEO

So . . . four months later, Geo calls and we make plans for our first date.

He shows up with a **toaster oven** in one hand and an **extra pair of socks** in the other. And we hadn't even slept together.

Spot pulls me aside and says, "What's he planning to do? Toast all our bread?"

After he plugs in the toaster oven, we go to a birthday party at our neighbor Orson Bean's house. (Orson Bean, the legendary actor and raconteur, who's also on *Desperate Housewives* and lives across the canal alley with his actress wife, Alley Mills.)

It's a pretty good party, "although not as good as the last one," I comment to Geo, "where everybody got fall-down drunk, while Orson stood around in the rain *slappin' hotdogs on a grill*—**naked**—*except for a robe.*"

"Well, he said it would be casual," Geo said. "But let's hope he's put on some clothes."

Sometime during the party, Geo and I slip out and walk down to the canal bridge at the end of the street where we can have some privacy. We talk about the trolls that inhabit the waters beneath us, who have probably followed me from Buck Creek, Missouri, and are guiding us in some unseen, yet prophetic way. Then we kiss for the first time, and the trolls approve.

He never goes home after that because he figures he already is **home.**

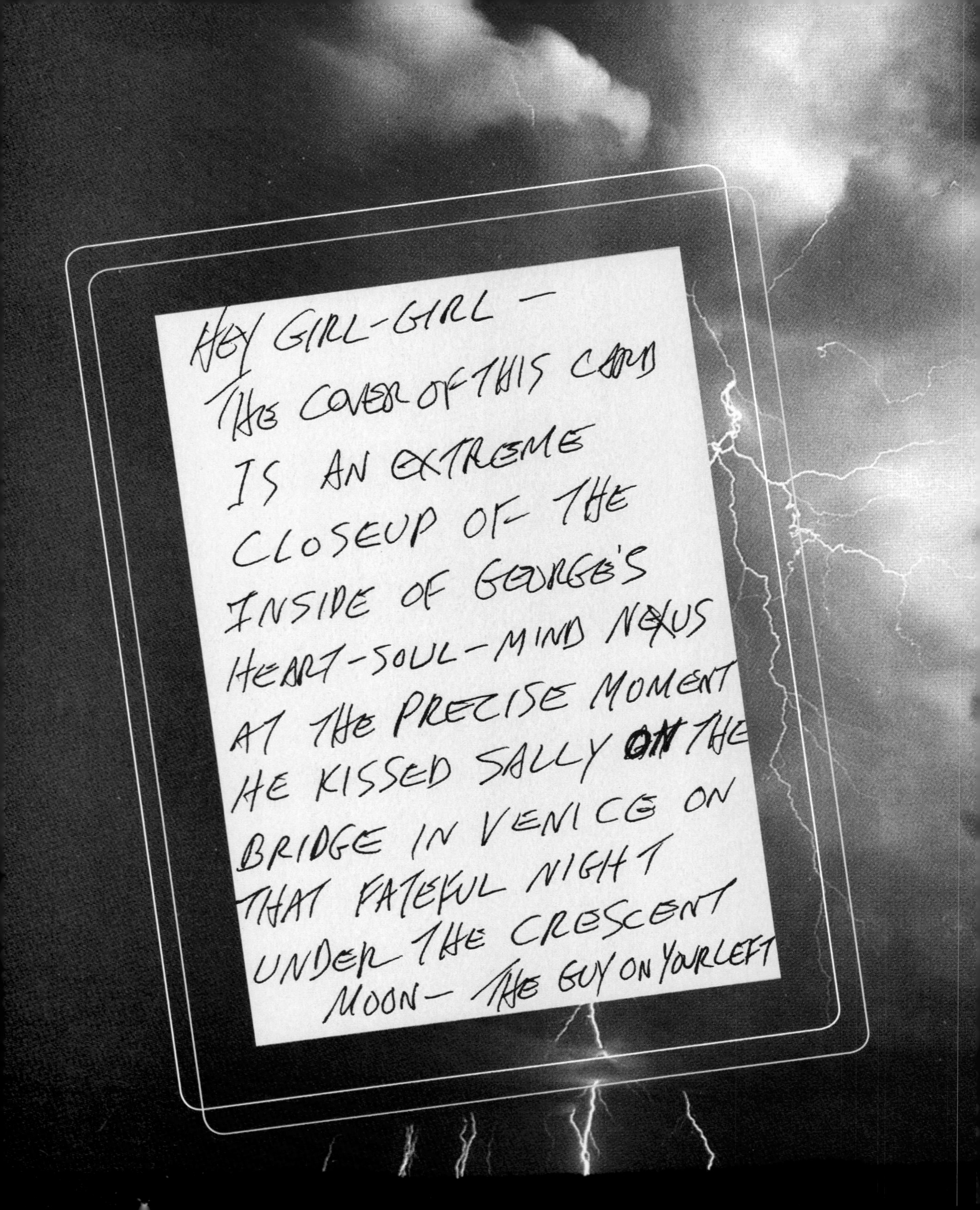

Hey GIRL-GIRL —
THE COVER OF THIS CARD
IS AN EXTREME
CLOSEUP OF THE
INSIDE OF GEORGE'S
HEART-SOUL-MIND NEXUS
AT THE PRECISE MOMENT
HE KISSED SALLY ON THE
BRIDGE IN VENICE ON
THAT FATEFUL NIGHT
UNDER THE CRESCENT
MOON — THE GUY ON YOUR LEFT

FOR THE GAL
WHO BROUGHT ME
TO THE CANALS....

...AND CHANGED MY LIFE.

CHAPTER 3

Geo Moves into the 'Hood

All hands on deck and batten down the hatches, there's a storm brewing on Linnie Canal. A hurricane, category five.

GEO MOVES IN

"He's Irish, you know," I overhear Spot saying to all the other dogs in the neighborhood.

When Geo moves to Venice,

everyone takes notice . . . including the paparazzi. One day, suddenly our picture is in the *Globe.* Not the *Boston Globe,* but the trashy *Globe*—where they always get at least two major things wrong. "And that's just in the caption," Geo says.

"The tabloid stories are loaded with lies," Spot adds.

"Just like your stories," he says to me.

"But fortunately we don't call them that, do we, Spotty?" Geo quickly adds, then bribes him with some of his chicken.

"No, we don't," Spot says, swallowing as he signals for more, then adds, "We call them 'a good story minus the facts.'"

In fact, Spot thinks Geo phones the *Globe,* the *National Enquirer,* and the *New York Post*'s Page Six, before we ever leave the house. "That's what the paparazzi who fell out of a tree told me. That's why I went ahead and sold him all those juicy details."

HURRICANE GEORGE

Everybody who's anybody from the Ozarks knows . . . **if you see a storm coming on the horizon, you've got to batten down the hatches.** Well, it's the same thing as having a man move in with you—you've got to prepare. Close the windows, lock the doors, dry-dock the boat, get ready for the coming storm. At first, I'm thinking: *I have to brace myself against real scary stuff, like* intimacy . . . *I've got to stake out my turf, strengthen my emotional barriers, reinforce my boundaries, and secure my independence.*

Hey Long and Pretty—
Some of the canal people had a *formal* meeting and unanimously voted Sally and George VENICE'S SWEET-EST LOVERS OF THE 20TH CENTURY. Also: BEST COMBINED 4 LEGS OF ANY COUPLE. Also: CUTEST ASSES. Also: BEST EYE-GAZING TWOSOME. Also: HORNIEST SEX TALKERS. Also: HOTTEST, JUCIEST MOUTHS IN EX-ISTENCE. Also: REGION'S GREATEST HUGGERS. Also: SOFTEST AND BEST STROKES AND TOUCHES all my love, till the last candle burns. CRYSTAL EYES G.

But instead of doing all that, I buy a new car (a BMW that looks suspiciously like his—both are black, except mine is the less expensive model), so Geo won't know I drive a clunker. And I show him my newly minted divorce papers, "without a speck of food on them," I point out. It's not like I'm trying too hard—or am I . . .

Sure, I'm a little nervous in the beginning of our relationship. And although I've always been in love with language the way he is, the first time we have lunch together, I have a pocketful of notes with clever stuff I've written on them, in case I run out of things to say. So, every now and then, I go into the ladies' room and pull out a note from my pocket, to see what I'm about to say next—a method I developed on stage whenever I forgot my lines. You know, something clever and spontaneous. In fact, it's so spontaneous, even I don't know what it is until I look at what I wrote. The lunch lasts more than three hours. **That's pretty damn clever and spontaneous if you ask me.**

ONCE GEO MOVES IN . . .

I can't walk down the street anymore without all the neighbors interrupting my thirty-minute interval training, wanting an autograph from Geo. Or neighbors like "Henry," wanting to know if they can have a cup of coffee with him. It's like having relatives who stick their noses in your marital business before the honeymoon's even over.

I gotta walk real fast . . . run, even. Although it hurts my knees. Spot thinks the diplomatic thing to do is to invite them over, let him drink coffee out of George Carlin's coffee cup—and charge him a couple of dollars.

"Well, Clinton did okay with the Lincoln bedroom. Why can't we do a little fund-raising with George Carlin's coffee cup?" he wants to know.

"What's it like living with such a big brain?" Henry asks. "That's some big brain he's got . . . !"

"I don't know, you'll have to ask him," Spot says.

That night, as I'm trying to go to sleep, I'm thinking of Geo, but picturing a **brain without any ears or nose or mouth**; instead—just a pair of eyeglasses on a skull that is resting on a cerebral cortex, which is sitting on a gullet. Just the visual image of it keeps me awake, making me feel guilty about all those chickens I beheaded in the Ozarks.

"Which was none," Spot reminds me.

True, but still it makes me feel guilty. Gives me scary nightmares too. Now bedtime's like a horror movie because of Geo's big brain, and I gotta sleep with the lights on. Spot, on the other hand, sleeps like a baby.

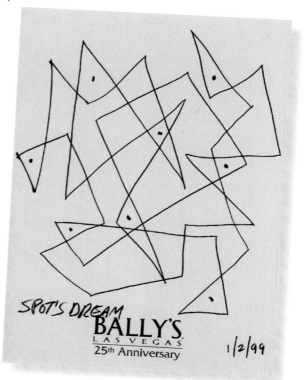

Geo's drawing of Spot's dream

WHAT DOES SPOT THINK ABOUT GEO MOVING IN?

"Why can't we do a little fund-raising with George Carlin's coffee cup?"

At first, Spot thinks Geo is a busybody. A common garden-variety busybody, hell-bent on destroying Spot's relationship with his owner by taking me away from him. He doesn't like it at all; Geo insinuating himself between us, compromising our tight-knit bond, and he says so.

"Step-dogs," I say to Geo. "You know how they complain. . . . They don't need any other reason than 'he's not the real title holder.'"

"Check my certificate of purchase," Spot says. "There's nothin' on there that says 'Carlin.'"

| LONG PEE
(12 SECONDS)

| REASONABLY
DECENT
SIZED
SHIT!!

Spot has Geo charting his bathroom breaks.

GEO TO SPOT: "Come on ya little turd bucket." He puts him on a leash. "You wanna be pals? Let's go for a walk."

SPOT TO GEO: "Okay but the next time you talk to me, address me as 'The Wise One,' not 'Hey, how goes it? Stop bein' a moron dog,' or 'Turd Bucket.' Those aren't ones I know . . ."

WHAT DOES GEO THINK ABOUT MOVING IN?

As he says in this card, *"They always hold hands or have their arms around each other—and they steal kisses—long ones and short ones—all along the way . . ."*

2511 — Concrete Pier, Santa Monica, California.

SARAH

The crowds have gathered on the pier to watch as Sally & George complete the first half of their DAILY walk from pier to pier — Venice to Santa Monica & back. They always hold hands or have their arms around each other — and they steal kisses — long ones & short ones — all along the way. Sometimes their feet get wet as a stronger wave washes up on them. They laugh and jump out of the way and kiss.

I love you, darling. Georgie

And it's **true.**

WHAT DOES SAL THINK ABOUT GEO MOVING IN?

Well, so much for battening down the hatches. After all that talk about bracing myself for the category five hurricane that is George Carlin—you know, all the stuff about drawing boundaries and fortifying my independence—it all went out the window as you can see in this email from Sal to Geo.

| Reply | Reply All | Forward | Delete | Previous | Next | Close |

```
hi baby,
i love you more than words can reveal.  i want to tell you that last night you cut
through all my defenses and penetrated my patterns of conditioning and went straight
into soul.  it felt like my brain patterns were interrupted and rechanneled into
something bigger and more loving than i've ever experienced or even dreamed of
experiencing.  in fact,  it was the greatest moment of my life.  what we represent
to each other -- me to you -- and you to me -- is more than any words -- other than
jupiterian -- can ever express.  let's celebrate forever.

i love you from beyond, beneath, and above the bridge,
sweet sara jane
```

So, Sal's happy . . .
Sal's in love.

So is Geo.

But Spot?

Meh

Sal tells Geo:

My stuff's always gonna be a mess! Where are you gonna put your stuff?

Geo tells Sal:

As long as you got a *"clear spot"* in the middle of it, my stuff will fit.

A clear Spot

CHAPTER 4

Day-to-Day *Stuff*

Speaking of stuff! You want to know what George Carlin does with *all his* **stuff** when he moves in with me? Well, he dumps it in the living room, dumps it in the bathroom, dumps it in the dining room—then expects me to figure out what to do with it. Although highly organized, there's a lot of **stuff.** There are boxes of **stuff** all over the bed, the floor, the table, the garage, the kitchen cabinets, the closets—sometimes even in the refrigerator. He moves my **stuff** to the back, and moves his junk to the front because, he says, **"his stuff is stuff and my stuff is junk."**

Then he throws my shit out. "It's junk," he says. "Let's get rid of it." Once I do, I notice he's keeping all his junk. "Well," he says, "my junk is good shit!" But even though it's all highly organized, his good shit still looks like junk to me. And by this time, all my good **stuff** is gone. Hauled off by the Monday-morning trash collectors.

Spot guarding my good shit

He not only has stuff everywhere—in every drawer, on every shelf—he also has extra stuff: a ten-year supply of pens, twenty years' worth of toilet paper, and stacks and stacks of tissue boxes. But he doesn't call this extra stuff **"too *much* stuff,"** like I do, he calls it **"surplus stuff,"** so that we won't run out.

He also brings his maid along to straighten his **stuff** up. Her name is China. And although I never thought I'd say this about another woman, she's not subservient enough. Once, when I specifically told her not to, she washes a white sweater of mine with a turquoise nightgown. Now I've got a white nightgown. I can't find the sweater, but I'm pretty sure it's turquoise.

In fact, she leaves my wet clothes on top of the dryer or in the garage on a makeshift broomstick clothesline. Whereas Geo's are in the closet, neatly folded and packaged with tissue paper in between the boxer shorts and T-shirts with holes in them that he wears at night for the air-conditioning effect. She doesn't wash them, she just irons them. **"Dirty, but ironed,"** Spot concurs. "From the way they smell."

She cleans the house piecemeal—one room per week. One week she'll do the bedroom, organizing the chest of drawers by taking everything out and putting it back, with Geo's clothes in the top two drawers, and mine in the bottom two. And once when she makes the bed, she leaves an ass print right on my pillow.

That's right, an **ass print** on my pillow.

I took a picture of it to show it to Geo when he got home. Spot says he didn't do it, so that leaves her, I point out.

The next week she'll do the kitchen. And I don't know what she thinks the sponge by the sink is for—I tell Geo she must think it's a birth control device, 'cause all she does is dick around with the dishes.

One week she washes the walls, but not the floor—so instead of eating off the floor at dinnertime, like we usually do, when I complain to Geo, he suggests we eat off the walls.

"Minor inconvenience in the scheme of things," Geo says optimistically, trying to prove that his decision to hire her was a good one. "Ya just gotta use plenty of stickum on the bottom of your plate. Paper plates work best. And don't fill your glass too full because refills can be troublesome."

"Wine's okay," Spot adds, "as long as you don't mind licking it off the floor."

"I don't," Geo says. "And neither does Spot, god bless him."

The maid also puts out these little air freshener things to make the house smell good, and we have to open all the windows in order to breathe.

"What are those called?" I ask, wanting to make sure I don't accidentally buy them myself.

"Little air freshener things," he says.

Then the neighborhood cat wanders in off the street. Takes one sniff, falls over dead.

"Did you know Orson Bean has thirteen cats?" I ask.

"Well, twelve . . ." Geo says.

TALKING TO THE NEIGHBORS, WITH SPOT BY OUR SIDE . . .

GEO: First thing Spot does is get up in the morning, smell some cat's asshole, then he goes in the yard and takes a dump. You couldn't ask for a better life than that!

SAL: No, even if you were a dog!

HEY HOT BOX—
GEORGE COOKS PASTA AT SALLY'S HOUSE AND ACCIDENTALLY IN- CLUDES A SMALL CAT IN THE SAUCE. HE CLAIMS THE RECIPE SAID:

4 TOMATOES CHOPPED
3 CLOVES GARLIC
1/4 CUP FRESH BASIL CHOPPED
3 TBSP. OLIVE OIL
1 SMALL CAT
MIX, COOK, EAT
PUKE

Salsville,
You are the girl of my dreams the queen of my heart the mistress of my des tiny and the CO-TENANT of my soul. I give myself to you fully — and eternally
THE CARLIN LAD

Speaking of taking a dump, George rarely failed to mention onstage that he swam in raw sewage when he was a kid to immunize himself against germs. "Go germs!" he'd say. But what he failed to mention is that at home, when we have stray ants in the kitchen, he tackles the problem head on by liberally spraying Black Flag Ant & Roach Killer—Pine Scent. It lasts fourteen days, then you gotta refresh your kitchen—all along the floor, around the door, all the way up the kitchen sink, and over the dirty dishes that "have to be washed anyway," he says. This is why I never cook at home.

One day, I find out his Afrin Nasal Spray works better than Raid. I know this because I see **high ants partying** all over his used Kleenexes, then falling over dead. I point out that Afrin is a dual bargain—it unclogs his nose and kills any stray ants angling for his turkey sandwich. "More for the dog," he says, and gives Spot a bite.

In fact, Geo is so at war with God's pesky creatures, that in between Larry King and Dr. Oz on his speed dial, he has an **opossum trapper who also deals with raccoons.** A "twofer," he says. The trapper actually traps the opossums from the crawl space beneath our house and moves them back into the wilderness, as opposed to killing them. Then we live possum-free for six or seven months, before, like homing pigeons, they find their way beneath our house again, waiting for another boxed lunch and a trip back to the wilderness—preferably with a stop at Starbucks along the way, like "Sally and Spot," here.

Geo is very impressed by the trapper not killing the opossums, and Spot is too. "They have just as much of a right to live here as we do," Spot points out. "In fact, they were here first—like the Indians."

"They might've even been here before the Indians," Geo says.

"Yeah, maybe the Indians stole the land from the opossums," Spot says. "It's possible!"

SALLY—
If you see me eyeing your kitchen too closely ~~immediately~~ PLAN A VACATION. IMMEDIATELY!

"Sally and Spot are seen here exiting Starbucks"

"And maybe the opossums stole the land from the raccoons," Geo says. "That's possible too."

Meanwhile, Geo thinks fake rocks with keys hidden in them fool burglars. I know this doesn't sound plausible, but even a *world-class* **embellisher** *like me* can't make this stuff up. Geo places a Hide-a-Key fake rock with an extra house key *under* the doormat by the front door. "Real obvious with the mat bulging like that," Spot says. "It doesn't even look like a rock"—thus making his job of guarding the house doubly difficult. When I tell Geo, "It's too obvious," he disappears, comes back, and says, "There. Now it looks like it belongs."

I still don't know where he put it. Hopefully in the trash . . .

People always ask me what's it like living with George Carlin.   Well, actually our conversation is so stimulating, it's hard to find a good time to go to the bathroom; I don't want to miss anything. As you can see from these notes Geo writes—Spot feels the same way. . . .

They call him "30-Second Spot." He goes out to have a pin + he's back in 30 seconds.

MISS PEE ~~PEE~~ IS LEAVING THE ROOM .,., AGAIN.

SALLY SURPASSES ~~HER~~ PREVIOUS PERSONAL BEST WITH TWO PEES WITHIN 6 MINUTES.

At our house, we rarely socialize so we have no sofa, only office chairs in the living room, so that company won't get comfortable enough to stick around. There are a couple of bar stools in the kitchen that look uncomfortable enough to make you want to stand. We have a dining room table, but it's piled high with Geo's stuff so you can't really use it. And there's no extra bed in the guest room, or my mother would want to come and stay. And we can't have that. **"Stopping by is one thing, staying is another,"** Geo adds.

In the morning, Geo, being task-oriented and all, brings me iced tea and a muffin and the *New York Post*. In the afternoon, he brings Spot, who's an aficionado of pop culture, a *Vanity Fair* (if it's out), and the latest gossip magazines—including the ones with aliens and flying saucers. And at night, he brings me apple pie from the health food restaurant, four small Tootsie Rolls (or else I'd eat the whole bag), and tears out the Daily Jumble from the *L.A. Times* for me to fill out later.

HOW GEO WAKES SAL UP

Geo wakes up before I do, enters the room, and says, "Wake up! America has been led astray by the cash register, the credit card, and the mall! The marketers have sucked the spirit out of American life! What's next? Chocolate-flavored condoms? Tasers in leopard print? How about medical marijuana from vending machines? Or a 'Tooth Tunes,' a toothbrush that plays music?"

"There are too many choices!" Geo continues, making sure Sal's awake. "Ordering coffee used to be simple: 'Gimme a cuppa coffee!' Now, not only is there a Starbucks on every corner, but I'm waitin' for them to put one in my colon so I don't have to go that far!"

IT'S MORNING. TIME FOR THE WORLD TO DEAL WITH THE AMAZING, MAGNIFICENT, WONDERFUL SALLY WADE

SAL— I Love You, YOU BEAUTIFUL, SEXY, POWERFUL WOMAN. I WILL BE WITH YOU FOREVER YOUR MAN G

And when I ask him why he wakes me up when I tell him not to, he says, "I was just walking by when I saw your eye open." He figured that one eye opening was enough. But my eye opened because he was walking by, so I say, "No. It needs to be two eyes." Then, once he notices both eyes are open, he leaves the room saying, "Okay, now I need to take some time for me."

After a while, I start getting up at the same time he does. He goes on antidepressants because of that. Says it ruins his "alone time."

As a matter of fact, we both notice that if two people are doing their morning routines together, it doesn't work as well, because each makes comments along the way and the interruptions start to pile up and become irritating. I'm not sure antidepressants even work for that. So finally, I think, *what the hell, I'll sleep late again and that'll cure his depression!* The problem is, by the time I get up, ready for *my* "alone time" to gather my thoughts, he's ready to talk about all the stuff he's done already while I was sleeping.

And it's *a lot of* **stuff.**

BABY—
I'M REALLY SORRY
I WOKE YOU UP.
THAT FUCKIN' DOOR LATCH
SOUNDS LIKE A HAMMER.
I WANTED TO LET YOU
SLEEP & I KNOW YOU'RE
MAD. I WAS TRYIN' TO
GET OUT QUIETLY.
I LOVE YOU
GEO

Sal, using a "Tooth Tunes" toothbrush

Reply   Reply All   Forward   Delete   Previous   Next   Close

IT'S A WOOONDERFUL MORNINGGGG!   IIIIT'S A BEAUTIFUUUL DAY!   THINKING ABOUT YOU INNN THE
MOOOOORNING!   MAKES FOR A WOONDERFUL DAAAY!

SJ

E-mail from Sal to Geo

GEO'S MORNING SPOT REPORT

- QUIET ALL MORN-
  ING
- HAPPY, GLAD TO SEE
  ME, BUT CONTENT
  IN GARAGE
- PEE + CHICKEN
  1st TIME OUT (5:05AM)
- SLEEPS IN DINING
  ROOM
- VOLUNTARY POOP AFTER
  NAP. (WHEN YARD DOOR WAS OPEN)
  NO CHICKEN.

②

- SPRAYED IN MOUTH FOR
  EATING PILLOW
- ATE FOOD AT 8AM,
  DOOR LEFT OPEN,
  2ND VOLUNTARY POOP
  AT 8:08 AM

  "GOOD BOY! GOOD BOY!"
  PIECE OF CHICKEN.

- SPRAYED IN MOUTH FOR
  SELECTING CASSETTE +
  RUNNING OFF WITH IT.
  8:15

Geo likes to take his time with
the newspaper, read blogs, check e-mails, plus he has long
lists of chores he organizes not only for himself, but he even
figures out my to-do list. How organized is *that*? He puts all
my appointments on his calendar, expecting me to put his
on mine, and when I don't, he's surprised by that. I'm not,
but he is.

Geo's lists are pretty impressive. And a lot of what
he does is for me. In fact, most of what he does on those
lists is for me. Which makes it so hard to complain that,
eventually, I go on antidepressants too.

THE DOGS WERE FED
AND I'M OFF TO DO
SOME SEQUENTIAL ♡
TASKING (AS OPPOSED
TO "MULTI-") AND I'LL
STAY IN TOUCH.
TEA TO COME ✓
POST TO COME ✓
MUCH LOVE + SMOOCHIES
♡   GEO. ♡

HIYA— BEE BEE
~~9:30~~ — 9:15
LEAVING
FOR
COFFEE
WITH
KEL

MR BUSY

Coffee with his daughter, Kelly, who has an irrepressible sense of humor

Geo also likes to narrate his progress through his lists. In fact, he announces everything he does to Sal before he does it, while he's doing it, and after he's done it. Even minutiae. Or rather, especially minutiae. For example, as Geo goes about his tasks, he announces,

"I'm gonna cross the room now, and I'm gonna pick up that dog bowl and I'm gonna fill it with water. Then, I'm gonna set it back down, walk across the room, sit down in front of my computer, take a sip of Diet Coke, and do a little more work on my suicide bit. It's not long enough yet. It's only fifteen minutes."

I'm not sure if I should applaud, or hum to block out the chatter. Instead, I say, "Yeah, no one's gonna want to kill themselves if the 'suicide bit' is only fifteen minutes long. Better make it twenty." Then, we both go back to being separately productive—but together.

In the evening, we do very little socializing. We don't need to because we find our conversation so stimulating. Usually we just go to a movie, eat out, or watch TV. Our favorite TV shows (aside from baseball, football, and basketball) are *CSI*, all the British murder mysteries, *Desperate Housewives* and *Gilmore Girls* when they were still on. I can tell Geo likes the *Gilmore Girls,* even though he doesn't say so, because he quits working and says,

"Time for the *Gilmore Girls?*"

Angela Lansbury in afternoon reruns of *Murder, She Wrote* and *Seinfeld* are high on his list of favorites, too. That is unless, of course, we find some channel with dwarf bowling, competitive eating, or bum fights with TV commercials that show a guy taking a shit.

"Serious
Lovers.
Are
From
Jupiter"
By Sally Wade & George Carlin

CHAPTER 5

Jupiter Sal & Geo

Hey Brightness –

No star twinkles brighter
than your eyes;
No planet holds more wonder
than your mind;
No inter-stellar distance
matches the dimensions
of your soul – and

NO GALAXY IS VASTER
THAN MY LOVE
Love,
SPACEMAN Carlin

"I feel like I've graduated from the human race some time ago,"
Jupiter Geo says to Sal.
"I too have sized up this species and found it lacking,"
Jupiter Sal replies.

LET THE TRUMPETS SOUND ;
LET THE DRUMS ROLL .
LET THE WORD GO FORTH :
FROM THIS DAY FORWARD, ALL OF
CREATION AND ALL OF EXISTENCE
IN THE COSMOS SHALL BE CALLED
~~GREATER~~ JUPITERIA, AND SHALL
BE REIGNED OVER BY THEIR
MAJESTIES, QUEEN SAL AND
KING GEO, FOREVERMORE. SO
SAY I, THE ~~HEAD~~ MOTHERFUCKER !!

From the beginning, we know we're from Jupiter. We call ourselves *Jupiterians,* because that's where we're from originally. Our lives here on Earth are meant to be spent exploring life downwind of Venus and Mars. It's a sacrifice both of us are willing to make, for the sake of our home planet. We keep an ongoing journal called **"Jupiter's Journal"** to chronicle our experiences, and each evening, pass a pad of paper back and forth, writing adventure love stories, all about the crazy things happening to us here on Earth, so that we can file an official report back on Jupiter.

And although George Carlin is all about the individual, Geo and Sal are like a set of matching bookends. And fortunately for us, according to Spot, "Two halves make one whole stable person." So at least we have that going for us.

We never enter a revolving door in separate compartments; we always go through together. With both of us shuffling our feet as quickly as possible, arms wrapped around each other, we call it, "Doin' the RIHGA Royal Shuffle!"—named after the New London Hotel, when it used to be called the RIHGA Royal Hotel, which is the first hotel we stayed at together in New York City.

We call ourselves twins.

The Jupiter Twins.

And we're a mighty force of nature.

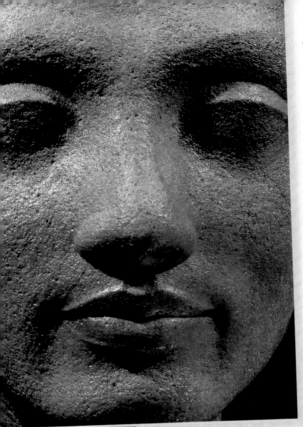

PEOPLE WE DON'T LIKE ARE FROM SATURN

We believe all Saturnians exert an evil influence over the world. To a Jupiterian, those from Saturn are known for being ignorant and lazy—there's a lot of prejudice and hatred between the two species . . . not to mention paranoia. In fact, there was a time when we wondered if Mr. Rogers was an evil Saturnian sent here to upset the eco-system and spy on we Jupiterians. He'd have been a likely choice—invisible to the untrained eye, seemingly innocuous . . . that's how they trick ya.

"Let's face it," I say to Geo one day, "Saturnians are a karmic mess. Plus, when they bring us our food, it's always cold."

"I guess keeping all that debris together in orderly rings must be difficult," he says.

"Definitely a sign of ORD (Obsessive Ring Disorder)," I say.

THEY DEFY DESCRIPTION. SO HERE GOES :

THE JUPITER TWINS ARE A MIGHTY FORCE OF NATURE, ROAMING THE SOLAR SYSTEM, SPREADING LOVE, HOLDING HANDS, WALKING GOOFY, EATIN' DESSERTS, WATCHIN' SUNSETS, KISSIN' ON BRIDGES, BLOWIN' BUBBLES, SCARIN' TROLLS, WISHIN' ON THE MOON, SNIFFIN' FLOW-ERS, FINDIN' MONEY AND SHARING A DEEP, SWEET ABIDING LOVE THAT LIGHTS THE UNIVERSE WITH A WARM, WARM GLOW. GEO

SAL

THE GREAT STONE FACE HAS SEEN MANY THINGS: IT HAS SEEN MOSES, CHRIST, BUDDA AND MOHAMMED; IT HAS SEEN THE BRITISH NAVY, NAPOLEON'S ARMIES AND THE UNITED STATES AIR FORCE; IT HAS SEEN YO-YO'S, HULA HOOPS AND STARBUCKS ———— BUT !! ...

IT HAS NEVER SEEN THE LIKES OF THE JUPITER TWINS. NO ONE HAS THEY SURPASS ALL EXPERIENCE; THEY TRANSCEND ALL COMPREHENSION; THEY CAN LEAP TALL BUILDINGS AT A SINGLE BOUND.

Mars, on the other hand, is okay. And so is Venus, which is where most dogs come from. Spot is a Venusian—although, he can pass as a Jupiterian . . . not unlike people from New Jersey who say they're from New York when they're away from home—sometimes it's just easier to shorthand it that way. At one time, Spot was actually thinking about opening a hot dog stand on Mars for those going to and from the Dog Star Sirius, but he hasn't gotten around to it yet. Venusians tend to get egotistical and lethargic unless you ply them with pizza and booze.

On Jupiter, we have our own modus operandi . . .

THE SINGLE LAW ALL JUPITERIANS ABIDE BY:

" <u>THIS IS THE LAW:</u>
FUCK 'EM ALL —
GOOD FOR US !"

THE THEME, MOTTO AND SUPER-AXIOM
FOR JUPITER'S ANGELS.

WANTED !!!

DOG MAN
— FROM
SATURN

<u>REWARD</u> !!!

SUBJECT BEFRIENDS
JUPITERIAN DOGS TO
GAIN ACCESS TO THEIR
HOUSEHOLDS TO HARASS
LOVING COUPLES.
BE ALERT, SPOT !

WHAT PEOPLE LOOK LIKE TO JUPITERIANS:

PEOPLE

WHAT SATURNIANS LOOK LIKE

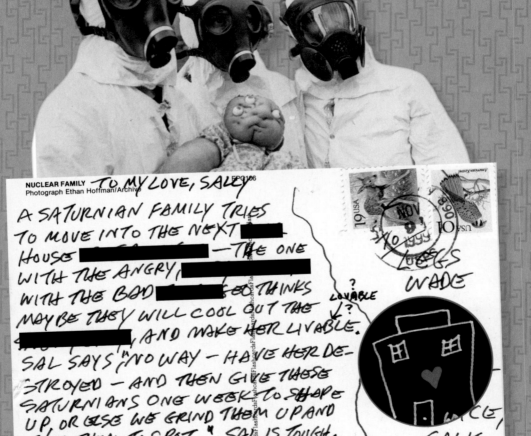

NUCLEAR FAMILY
Photograph Ethan Hoffman/Archive

TO MY LOVE, SALLY

A SATURNIAN FAMILY TRIES
TO MOVE INTO THE NEXT ████
HOUSE ████ ████ —THE ONE
WITH THE ANGRY ████████
WITH THE BAD ████ ███ THINKS
MAYBE THEY WILL COOL OUT THE
████ ████, AND MAKE HER LIVABLE.
SAL SAYS,"NO WAY — HAVE HER DE-
STROYED — AND THEN GIVE THESE
SATURNIANS ONE WEEK TO SHAPE
UP, OR ELSE WE GRIND THEM UP AND
FEED THEM TO SPOT." SAL IS TOUGH.

Flashcards™
"One is worth a thousand words"
Photographic Postcards
© Flashcards, Inc. 1986
781 West Oakland Park Blvd.
Fort Lauderdale, Fla. 33311
1-800-531-0777

FROM GEO.

GEORGE SUGGESTS A COM-
PROMISE: KILL ALL OF THEM
IMMEDIATELY AND GO TO CAPO
FOR THE TOMATO PLATE.

LOVABLE
↓ ?

?

LOVE,
WADE

NICE,
CALIF.
90291

(NOTE: This is an approximation only.)

The only three cults on Jupiter, to our knowledge:

CARLINTARIAN
MADETFARIAN
SALLYIST

CULTS
ON
JUPITER

The Jupiter Justice Department certifies all royal decrees—if Sal gets hungry, she may cash this in:

JUPITER JUSTICE DEPT.

THIS WILL ACKNOWLEDGE
THAT THE QUEEN MAY
HAVE ONE MORE SCONE
CORNER.

HRH
— REX
KING OF JUPITER

The four major food groups represented on Jupiter:	The Tootsie Roll, the gum drop, butterscotch, and another Tootsie Roll.

FOUND MONEY

One of the many things we do as Jupiterians, is save change we find on the ground. We call this "found money." To us, it's magic money and represents real change in our relationship. The higher the amount we find, the more significant the change. We open our first bank account with "found money" and never make withdrawals—only deposits—because someday we plan to do something significant, like retire in Jupiter, Florida. We'd never been there, but we liked the name of the town.

In Vegas, where Geo is headlining, not only do we go around picking up change on the ground, we even pull coins out of the fountains. In that New York—New York hotel, they have cameras everywhere and secret service men sometimes chase after us, so we duck out a side door.

The Jupiter Twins in Vegas (fresh from pulling coins out of the fountain)

NYC /AC /NYC MAR

SAT.	36¢		20
SUN.	—		21
MON.	5¢ - 5 PENCE		22
TUES.	78¢	1.24	23
WED.	27¢	1.51	24
THURS.	14¢	1.65	25
FRI.	.01¢	1.66	26
SAT	.00¢	1.66	27
SUN	.41¢	1.67	28

→ 10¢ IN NJ
TAK. BATHROOM,
1¢ IN NYC

The original 401K

We take copious notes

pages and pages recording
how much money we found
each day, each month, each
year—in pennies, nickels,
dimes, and quarters. In between
performances, Geo lists every
coin—in detail—where we found
it, the daily and monthly average.
When we made our first bank
deposit with that money, we're
talking a yield of more than a
couple hundred dollars a year.

"Or more," Geo adds.

Sometimes we hit three or four
7-Elevens in a row to see if we can find
coins under the counter. We go in as a team—one of us
distracting the clerk with a question, while the other leans
down and clears out whatever's on the floor nearby.

GEO KEEPS TABS: A SAMPLE WEEKLY TOTAL

1999   1999

rom Key West–LA

06–03	
07–00	
08–10	
09–01	
10–00	
11–00	
12–26	
13–20	
14–26	8 separate coins, most finds: 7
15–35	
16–01	
17–02	
18–00	
19–02	
20–10	
21–02	
22–79	
23–08	
24–36	
25–01	Travel day LA– NYC 5 cents, 5 finds
27–55	18 Separate finds; 43 cents after dinner, Il Mulino; 42 cents subway-related; instincts rule! First day all 4 denominations found.
28–01	
29–01	
30–15	
31–02	

JANUARY TOTAL: $ 3.85
JANUARY AVERAGE: $ 12.42 CENTS PER DAY

Sal, laughing all the way to the bank

Sweet SARAH—
My BODY GOES TO
LAS VEGAS —

MY HEART STAYS HERE.

JUPITER GEORGE
(SALLY'S GUY)

NICKNAMES— *Or How to Identify Us When We're Undercover*

As Jupiterians, we have many nicknames. I call him "Pie Pie," "Little Geo'gie," or else I call him the "Big Baby." I also call him "Grumpy Dick, the City Hick," and he calls me "Coconut Mallory the Country Slicker." Together, we're "The City Hick and Country Slicker, Jupiter Geo and Jupiter Sal." I'm "Cookie" and he's "Cake." We're several hundred people; we're the entire population of Jupiter. That's why in the white pages of the phone book on Jupiter, they have fifty thousand names, but it's all the same number.

JUPITER DUTY ROSTER *(LIST 4 PET NAMES)*

MORNIN' COOKIE!!

TWO HEARTS

SAL + GEO
SARAJANE + GEORGIE
GOOFY 1 + GOOFY 2
COOKIE + CAKE
SALLY + GEORGE

HOTEL MAN

I ! LOVE !! YOU !!!)

" HEY, TEA BAG!"

" WHAT, COFFEE CUP?"

A LIST OF PET NAMES:

GEO & SAL:

CRABBERS AND GRUMPS

COCONUT MALLORY AND GRUMPY DICK

MR. AND MRS. ZIPLOCK

POOKENHEIMER & PEEKENMEISTER

POOKIDOODLEDOO & POODLEDEDUM

POOK-A-LOONIE & PEEK-A-LITO

COOKS & CAKES

CAKEALATOR & COOKIFIER

THE COOKILATIN' BABYLATOR SALLIGATIN' WADE & THE CAKEIFIED STUDAGATOR GEORGIFYIN' CARLIN

THE CAKEAFILATIN' HAPPIFIER & THE STUDILATIN' KISSAMAKER

PUSALLY & COCKARLIN

BIIIIIIIIG BEE-BEE & BEE-BEE BEE-BEE

GEO:

MR. EMPHATIC A.K.A.
RUBBERBANDMAN

SEÑOR NUEVA YORK

HIS ROYAL STRANGENESS

THE MAN YOU ASTONISH

MR. ME

THE G-MAN

YOUR GUY, GEO

EDITOR-IN-CHIEF

BIG GEO ON THE CANALS

LOVER BOY

CRUSTY

JUPITER GRUMPS

HIS ROYAL SOMETHING OR OTHER

STAGE STUD

YOUR POWERFUL LOVE

CUPCAKE CARLIN

YOUR MYSTERIOUS BENEFACTOR
WITH GREAT LOVE AND HOT PANTS

MR. TINKLE DICK

MR. DONUT

SAL:

THE BAGEL BUNNY

KEEPER OF THE FLAME

SARRY MY HEART

THE SWEAT LADY

SISTER SALLY WADE

COCONUT MALLORY

ESS-JAY

THE GIRL IN MY HEART

THE LADY WALKING THE DOG

THE PEARL OF MY HEART

HEAT

LIGHT

DARLIN' GIRL

SARA

THE RECENT MRS. CARLIN

SPOT:

THE COCKER IN THE YARD

LITTLE BEE-BEE

ONE MORE FACTOID ABOUT SATURNIANS WE THINK YOU SHOULD KNOW!

They not only eavesdrop on Jupiter Sal and Geo, they sow dissent by discouraging our quest for coins; thereby trying to bankrupt us and compromise our ability to fight the good fight against evil and prevent us from changing. "They want to stop our growth and we want to blow 'em out of the universe," says Jupiter Geo. So on days when our take is low, we know it's the Saturnian influence.

WE WROTE JUPITER STORIES EVERY EVENING, TRADING THE NOTEPAD BACK AND FORTH. THESE ARE A FEW EXAMPLES.

On the Way to Fix the Printer:
A Jupiter Story

Written in Las Vegas, Nevada, by **Jupiter Geo** *and* **Sal**

Sal: Geo drove down Las Vegas Boulevard in his 4-wheeler, tryin' to outrun 4 cops on bicycles with radios because he had some "smoke" in his pocket. "Smoke" meaning wood burning oven pizzas from Spago's that were hotter than hell.

Sparks flew from his window, catching all of Treasure Island on fire, while tourists scrambled for ropes from which to swing from windows.

Geo: Sal saved two people from Iowa and they rewarded her

60

with a free trip to Spain. Sal & Geo took a rain check because they had to meet ol' Freddie Fuck-eye who was gonna fix their printer.

Sal: But before that, Geo signals Sal with a walkie-talkie that was attached to the computer CD Rom, outrunning the cops in a high speed chase—who had ordered backup highway patrolmen & called in the National Guard. Intercepting the CD Rom message were a group of . . .

Geo: . . . German NATO soldiers who were in town for some Chinese food. Sal sent them to Chang's just to get even for what Germany had done in the Second World War. One of the soldiers offered her some Beano, which she took for Jupiter Geo.

Sal: Back to the chase.

tryin to
Outrunning
the cops in A
high speed chase
who had ordered
back up high way
Patrolmen & called
in the national
Guard. Intercepting
the C.D. Rom
message were
A group of German NATO
SOLDIERS who were
in town for some
Chinese food. Sal
sent them A CHANG'S
just to get even for
WHAT GERMANY had
done in the Second
World War. One of
the soldiers offered
her some BEANO which
she took for JUPITER
GEO. BACK to the
chase.

WITH A free trip t
Spain. Sol & GEO took
a rain-check be-
cause they had t
meet OL' FREDDIE
FUCK-eye who was
gonna fix their printer.

But before that,
GEO signal Sal
with a walkie
talkie that was
attached to the
computer CD Rom

The ~~pizza~~ hot wood-burning pizza was beging to cool down. because GEO had licked the cheese off the crust. But the officers still detected "SMOKE" enough for a 20-lifetime prison sentence

Finally, ~~S~~ she who was circling the city in the latest Jupiterian-style ~~quick~~ streetm ~~ship~~ spotted him as he was being frisked and billy-clubbed ~~by~~ at the side of the road. She PRESSED THE CRYSTAL-ACTIVATION BUTTON,

~~of~~ GEO's hand ~~Boosting~~ ~~billing him~~ into the Spacecraft along with his four wheels ~~and they sped~~ ~~away~~

and they sped away into the night, past Venus, all the way to the moon. where they landed feet-first to renew

AND GEO'S CRYSTALS SPRANG TO LIFE IN HIS POCKET. THEY GAVE OFF A HORRIBLE ODOR THAT FELLED ALL 4 POLICEMEN; AS THEY LAY THERE, GEO TOOK .39¢ IN CHANGE OUT OF THEIR POCKETS, AND SOME OREOS THAT WERE STRAPPED TO THE BIKES FOR EMERGENCIES. THEN SHE SWOOPED DOWN AND GRABBED HOLD *their vows to love each other longer than forever.*

By the way — Treasure Island Burned — but was the only casualty.

END of Jupiter story

Although they must've rebuilt that ... thing in a hurry — cause this is the way it looks — now.

TREASURE island

The hot wood-burning pizza was beginning to cool down because Geo had licked the cheese off the crust. But the officers still detected "smoke"—enough for a 20-lifetime prison sentence. Finally, Sal, who was circling the city in the latest Jupiterian-style Gulfstream, spotted him as he was being frisked and billy-clubbed at the side of the road.

Geo: She pressed the crystal-activation button, and Geo's crystals sprang to life in his pocket. They gave off a horrible odor that felled all 4 policemen; as they lay there, Geo took .39 cents in change out of their pockets, and some Oreos that were strapped to the bikes for emergencies.

Sal: Then she swooped down and grabbed hold of Geo's hand, boosting him into the space craft along with his four-wheeler, and they sped away in the night, past Venus, all the way to the moon—where they landed feet-first and renewed their vows to love each other longer than forever.

Sal: By the way—Treasure Island burned—but was the only casualty.

Sal: Although they must've rebuilt that thing in a hurry—cause this is the way it looks now.

End of Jupiter Story . . .

"I'M COMPLETELY SWEPT AWAY BY YOU, US AND THE BUBBLE. IT'S MIRACULOUS — IT'S LIFE-SHIFTING

TOP FIVES

Writing "Top Fives" is a Jupiterian ritual at the end of the day. Sometimes we write our own . . .

And sometimes we write them together—about each other.

5 TOP THINGS ABOUT
GEO & SAL

1. HONESTY - intellectual and emotional

1A. LOVING CONCERN - for ME and for SPOT.

2. WILLINGNESS to LISTEN AND respond.

2A. SMART as 20 MOTHERFUCKERS! SMART, SMART, SMART! AND NOT JUST SMART —— WISE SMART.

3. HUMANITY AND VULNERABILITY that MAKE UP HIS SOUL. THE NOT - LEARNED OR LEARNABLE QUALITIES

3A. THE SWEET, STUNNINGLY BEAUTIFUL FACE THAT COMMUNICATES HER ~~MORE~~ POWERFUL, PRODIGIOUS LOVE.

4. Communicating bothersome Activities LiKE   1. Driving instructions
2. Jeans in bed
As well as HARDER things like
3. going through past memories and
4. feeling his "shell."

4A. CONSTANTLY EXAMINING OUR RELATIONSHIP IN A HEALTHY ATTEMPT TO HEAD OFF TROUBLE, AND TO PRESERVE OUR LOVE. WILLINGNESS TO RISK UNPLEASANT CONVERSATION for the SAKE OF IMPROVE-MENT.

5. SHINES WHEN A LOVE LIGHT IS ON HIM .. BEAMS WITH ENVIABLE JOY. DARKENS UNDER A CLOUD.

TOP 5   MON. 10/11
- HUGGING + KISSING SALLY
- LUNCH TOGETHER
- GETTING CHANYA + JACK STRAIGHTENED OUT (WINK, WINK, NUDGE)
- SEEIN' SPOT
- EVERYTHING RUNNIN' ON TIME

SOMETIMES WE DO
BOTTOM FIVES as well.

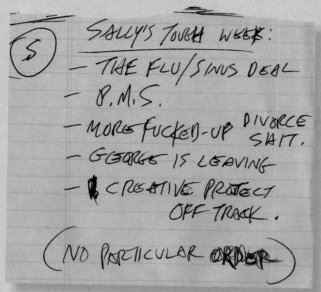

S SALLY'S TOUGH WEEK:
- THE FLU/SINUS DEAL
- P.M.S.
- MORE FUCKED-UP DIVORCE SHIT.
- GEORGE IS LEAVING
- CREATIVE PROJECT OFF TRACK.

(NO PARTICULAR ORDER)

Sal's written by Geo

TROLL'S BAD LIST

A. GUARDING BANANAS

B. MEDDLING WITH GEO AND BEIN' INSULTED.

C. NOT MUCH CONVERSATION IN CAL.

D. THREAT OF BEIN RETURNED TO THE OZARKS

Sal's inner troll's "Bottom Five"

Spot's BAD THINGS TODAY LIST

A. NO VALENTINES DAY CHOCOLATE.

B. NO BED HALF the DAY. (in garage)

C. Stuck in garage DURING dinNER.

D. SORE HIP, failing eyesight

E. SQUIRTED with brown GOO

GEO'S BAD THINGS TODAY LIST

A. PHONE BROKEN

B. 2 COMPUTERS BROKEN

C. 2 DEFECTIVE PARTS COME IN MAIL

D. CAR HIT + DENTED

E. GATE LOCK FUCKED UP

F. Ticket on Ford.

G. FIGHT - PICKED ON.

65

Time once again for another chapter of "DOWN BY THE BRIDGE," the story of two CRAZY LOVERS defying all odds AND USING JUPITER as a SHIELD against the NEGATIVE WORLD.

One more Jupiter story

Geo: *Time once again for another chapter of "Down by the Bridge," the story of two crazy lovers defying all odds and using Jupiter as a shield against the negative world.*

OUR FIRST STORY TOGETHER,
written in Key West, Florida.
"Night Night '98"

Sal: *The Balcony Babies dined at the rooftop restaurant under cloudy skies and gentle sprinkles. The moon shone brightly as Jupiter winked. They declared their . . .*
Geo: *. . . orders to the waiter and, soon after, found themselves chowing down and thinking lewd thoughts. After several desserts they walked sweetly home to confront the waning of the year—the best year of both their lives . . .*
Sal: *And the one that began with the Jupiterian influence that carries them perfectly through an imperfect world.*

OCEAN KEY HOUSE
SUITE RESORT & MARINA

①

"New years eve"

The Balcony Babies dined At the rooftop restaurant under cloudy skies and gentle sprinkles. The moon shone brightly as Jupiter winked. They declared their orders to the waiter and, soon after, found themselves chowing down and thinking lewd thoughts. After several desserts they walked sweetly home to confront the waning of the year—the best year of both their lives. And the one that began with the Jupiterian influence that carries them perfectly through an imperfect world.

Zero Duval Street, Key West, FL 33040 · Tel: 305.296.7701

(4)

SUDDENLY, IT WAS THE FOLLOWING
YEAR. TWO PREVIOUSLY LONELY PEOPLE WERE
ENTERING THE SECOND CALENDAR YEAR OF
THEIR NEWFOUND TOGETHERNESS — A SWEET
PAIRING OF TWO LOVING SOULS BENT ON
A LIFE TOGETHER.

Then fireworks exploded ~~and~~
BECAUSE
∧ George and Sally kissed on the
balcony. They illuminated the
sky, bursting into random
displays of stars, hearts and
lips. They shook the HEAVENS ~~sky~~ and
rattled the ground. all because
of the love two Jupiterians have for
each other. Night Night '98

Geo: *Suddenly, it was the following year. Two previously lonely people were entering the second calendar year of their newfound togetherness—a sweet pairing of two loving souls bent on a life together.*
Sal: *Then fireworks exploded because George and Sally kissed on the balcony. They illuminated the sky, bursting into random displays of stars, hearts, and lips. They shook the heavens and rattled the ground—all because of the love two Jupiterians have for each other tonight. Night night '98.*

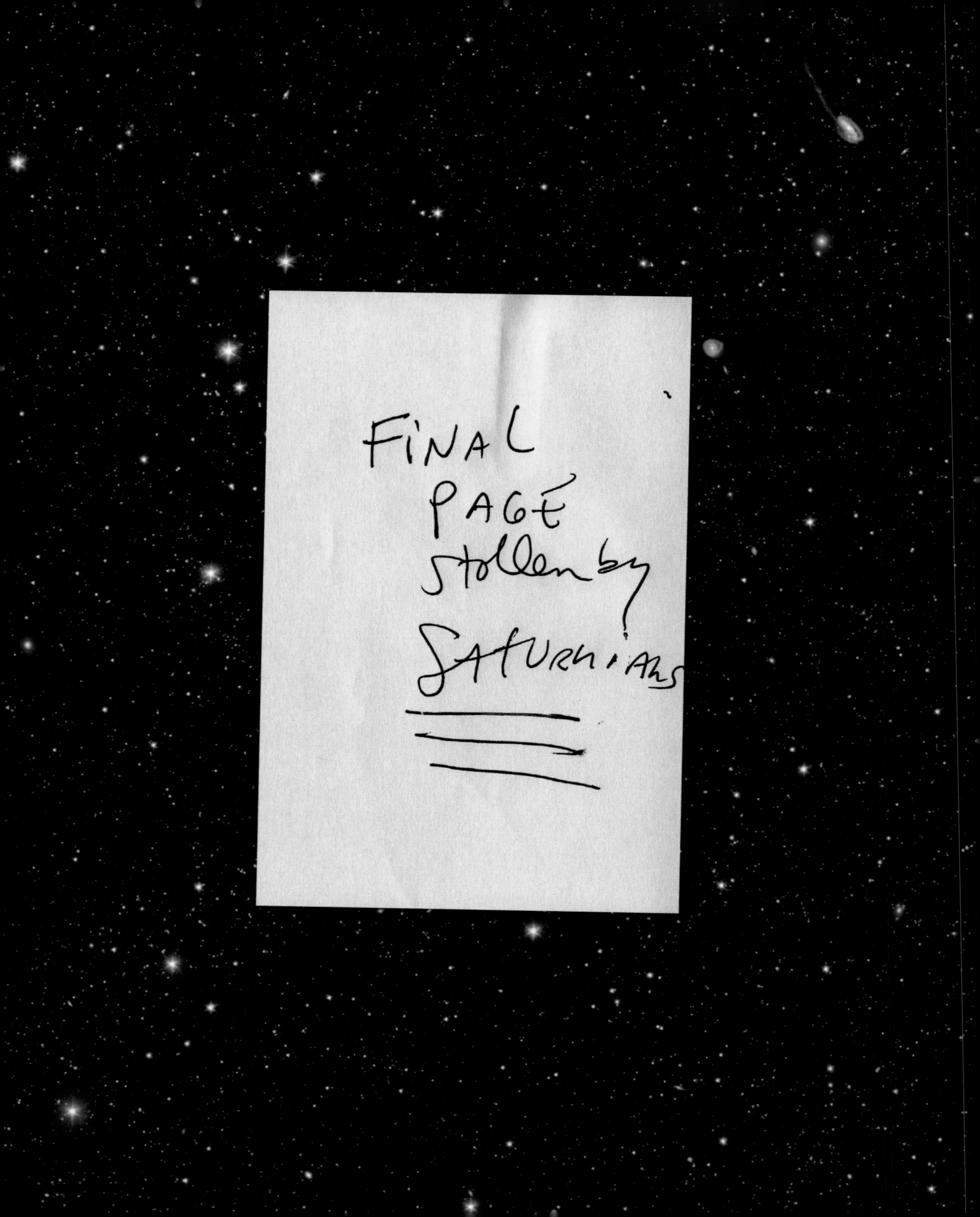

FINAL
PAGE
stollen by

SATURNIANS

I'M SILLY for SALLY

YOU KNOW HOW I feel ABOUT YOU? If you took all the words—on—paper ever written; times all the SYMBOLS ON TABLETS; times all the BYTES ON COMPUTERS, TIMES all the WORDS spoken — and multiplied it by itself, you still WOULD NOT come near expressing the number of ZEROES that would follow the number that represented my love — AND IT'S ALREADY PRETTY HIGH!!!

Neither Geo nor I are ordinary. As my friend once said to me, "There's a level you'd have to meet George on; you were evenly matched and he knew it."

I said to her, "Well, that's true. I mean, just because Geo had a better memory than I do, a better sense of humor and timing, a quicker wit, and a finger always on the pulse instead of the blow dryer, doesn't mean we weren't evenly matched. In fact, we sounded just alike."

That's the snow job I gave her. But the truth is, Geo's so good with words, he can do a *New York Times* crossword puzzle in the same length of time it takes Sal to just write down any ol' letters, regardless of what they spell. But Sal plugs along, sometimes taking the lead, making "our life together"—as Geo puts it—"just like the circus, the rodeo, the carnival, the sideshow, the parade, and the cavalcade all rolled into one."

There was another word after "cavalcade," but I can't remember what it was. Geo would know.

We call ourselves
"Crabby & Proud,"
"Grumpy & Loud,"
and have this note we wrote together taped to our refrigerator door.

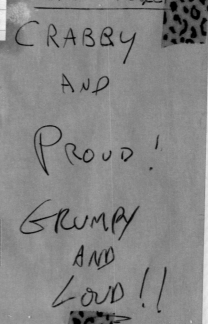

Geo & Sal
Bon Mots

Once when a doctor canceled my appointment, and I wondered if it was because he was mad at me, Geo said, "Let's assume the best—that his mother died."

SAL: What's the matter?
GEO (*frowning*): I keep havin' to go to the bathroom, then when I sit down, it's only a big fart!

SAL: Either I'm getting a huge chest or the maid keeps shrinking my bras.
GEO: Well, you know which one I'm rooting for.

SAL: Shall I tuck my shirt in?
GEO: Seein' how you slept in it—I can't see that it makes any difference.

SAL: You're a smarty-pants.
GEO: Smarty pants, smarty shirt . . .
SAL: No, you're only the pants, baby. Let's not get carried away.

Dashing through an airport, when Geo says, "Oh, blow me!"
SAL: I can't right now—we're in a hurry.
GEO: That's true.

71

GEO. SAID, "I GOT WRITER'S BLOCK," then "WRITE THAT DOWN," SHE SAID QUICKLY, "THEN IT'LL BE GONE," THAT MADE HIM THINK, "WHAT A BLOOMIN' GENIUS I GOT ON MY HANDS, HERE; SHE'S RIGHT. WRITIN' ABOUT NOT WRITIN' IS JUST RIGHT—RIGHT? IT OUGHTTA BE A RITE.

G YOU'RE DOIN' GREAT.
S YOU'RE GREAT. AND I'M DOIN' YOU. I'M DOIN' GREAT!

Geo: If I keep seeing my proctologist, he says I'll end up the perfect asshole.

Sal: Which way to Ben Nile's office?
Geo: Disarray.

Sal to saleslady about Geo: Geo has a large jean pool to choose from already. Three new pairs! That's why he doesn't want to buy any jeans.

Sal: You know what you are? A creative problem solver.
Geo: Yeah, 'cause if you think about something long enough, there's usually a way of gettin' around it.

Sal: I'd call my mother, but I don't really want to commit suicide today.
Geo: Well, maybe you can talk her into it!

Geo: Okay, right now I'm gonna go get my stool sample thing.
Sal: I don't really need that much detail.
Geo: I know, but I like to inform you.

Geo: I can never remember the stuff that doesn't make sense.
Sal: That's okay, I'll do it.

Sal: Bad mood?
Geo: I had messages, I had things to do, and I couldn't take a shit.

Geo: They don't make fuckin' people like you, Sal. You're a figment.

Sal: Really?

Geo: Yeah.

Geo: Telling me not to take you seriously is like telling an American soldier the Vietcong are just fooling around.

Sal: No one's ever compared me to the Vietcong before.

Geo: Another first for me.

Sal: I didn't fix my hair today.

Geo: If it ain't broke, don't fix it. It ain't broken.

Sal (*2:15 a.m., waking Geo up in the middle of the night*): You know what's great? When you wake up and find you still have six hours to sleep! (*Geo rolls over and goes back to sleep. Sal stays awake and thinks about how smart she is.*)

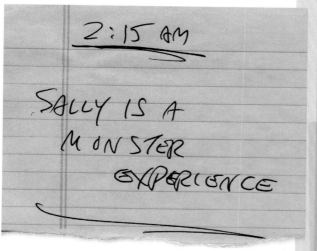

Sal: You're already the perfect everything— including asshole.

73

Sal to Geo: Your mind is so sharp, I'd like to shave my legs with it.

Geo's definition of bikini waxing: Throwin' your puss over your shoulders. As in "Go throw your puss over your shoulders, baby."

Sal explains why she puts powder on her forehead, in case Geo's interested....He is.
Sal: I keep doing that so my bangs won't get oily.
Geo: Talk about your chemistry major!

Sal: Why do guys leave the bathroom door open and pee with reckless abandon whenever ya dial the phone and it's too late to hang up?
Geo: I dunno. You scared the piss back up to my ears. I'll never pee again.

Sal (*using an old Ozarkian expression*): Pardon me all to hell and back in a handbasket!
Geo: Pardon me all back to hell in a basket of hands.

When I introduce Geo to a friend I call Guru Jack, because he's the happiest guy I know . . .
Geo: You must be horrible at funerals.

Geo: You're not here to run a race—you're here to dance a dance.
Sal: What do ya mean? You're the only guy I know who gets busy and takes a nap.

Geo: **You're not here to run a race— you're here to dance a dance.**

Sal: I just realized I'm lazy and didn't know that.

Geo: Yeah, that's because you've been covering it up all these years with activity.

Sal: Okay, I gotta go back to work now.

Geo: Oh no, you don't wanna fall into *that* trap.

Sal: I hate holidays. All the good restaurants are closed and you gotta drive forever to find a Starbucks that's open.

Geo: Well, fuck 'em—what do they know?

Sal: But how can everyone, everywhere, be out of town? If the streets aren't crowded anywhere, where has everybody gone?

Geo: There must be some city somewhere that's overrun with tourists, where nobody can get around.

When Geo and Sal are bored, depressed, and fed up with living in a Vegas hotel in 105-degree heat, Geo asks, "How, in an environment with no humidity and the pressures of work and maintenance of the bubble, can you still look fresh as a daisy?"

Sal: I don't know. How?

Geo: Because freshness and daisyhood come from the inside and they overpower environment and circumstances, no matter how hostile or trying.

Geo: He don't know dick!

Sal: He knows Jane, but not Dick!

Geo: I know Jane . . . Sarreee Jane.

Sal: What about Vim and Vigor, ever met them?

Geo: Yeah, they're brothers.

You are like a volcano that won't shut down. Keep spewin' out lava, baby!

LIVE HARD

Sal: This is the life!

Geo: Oh, really? I was thinking *that* was the life. And here I've been wrong all *this* time.

Sal to Geo: By the way, did you know that turkeys in Turkey are called Americans?

At a Chinese restaurant, when Sal asks Geo if he'd like to order moo shoo chicken, he says,

"When I go to a Chinese restaurant, I like to order flung dung."

Sal (*after a trip to the hair salon*): How do you like the color?

Geo: I think your hair has a simmering natural blondness now instead of a cheap California sheen. Before it glistened like the chrome bumper on a car. It was far more metallic looking.

Sal: Are all Afghanis the same age? I keep seeing this one guy in every truck that goes by, but he keeps changing guns.

Geo: I dunno. Write that down.

Sal: By the way, have you noticed that the people who instigate war always seem to take the weekends off?

Geo: No. But I've realized every man's gonna want to carry fissionable plutonium in his purse someday.

Geo (*walking arm in arm with Sal past Victoria's Secret in Vegas*): Did they ever find out what that was?

Sal: How do ya like that Spanish song?

Geo: I'm not really sure. They could be singin' about dismembering a baby for all I know.

A snippet of conversation about my mother . . .

SAL: My mother's coming today.

GEO: That's not my fault.

SAL: She'll be here at three.

GEO: I know that.

SAL: Well, now you know it twice!

Stopping at a gas station while traveling through Florida . . .

SAL: Where's the bathroom?

ATTENDANT: Back there.

SAL: Where, out back?

GEO: She's from the Ozarks.

Geo thinks it's funny, so he writes it down.

A joke we both came up with, twenty-eight years apart:

Peacock, peacunt . . . that's a female peacock.

When I asked Spot why Geo didn't laugh, Spot said, "It's because he'd already heard it."

So I changed mine:

A peacock in a peacoat is a peacunt.

~ Sally Wade

SAL: Whatcha doin'?

GEO: Gettin' the water outta the little cracks of my ears.

SAL: Are you gonna kiss me or are you gonna play with your feet?

GEO: Of course I'm gonna kiss you.

SAL: You made the right decision.

"WHERE'S THE BATHROOM?"

"BACK THERE?"

"WHERE, OUT BACK?"

"SHE'S FROM THE OZARKS"

peacock
peacunt.
that's a female
peacock.

Sal's note

"How can I remember better?"
Sal asked.
"I FORGET" Geo confided.

We're doin' okay for a couple of jackoffs.

Screw politics. Whatcha gonna eat?

Things Geo says to Sal frequently:

- CALM THE WOMAN DOWN
- IT DON'T MEAN DICK
- YA GOT POTENTIAL!
- WOWIE ZOWIE! YER A FUGGIN' GENIUS!
- FERK THAT
- HOLY MACARONI!
- WELL, WOOP-DE-DOO
- OKEY DOKEY, SMOKEY
- YOWSAH, BABY
- SPIFOLA, BABY
- TRUE 'NUFF
- HUBBA, HUBBA
- YER ALL RIGHT, BABY
- YER A KEEPER!
- (BURP)
- GETTIN' DROWZISH
- AWWWWW GEE
- YAAAAAAAYYY!!!
- ACHEWY!

- WHY I OUGHTTA . . .
- YOU'RE CUTER THAN AN ANT'S ASS
- BEEN THERE, DONE THAT, GOT THE T-SHIRT, WORE THE HAT!
- HEY, CHEER UP, YER IN LOVE!
- GIMME A KISS, GOOFY!

When do I get to talk?

Things Geo says to Sal infrequently:

- BOOYAY! *(Means tanked on tea . . .)*
- OLD SCARS ALWAYS HEAT UP THE CLIMATE
- YOU MAH HONEY!
- WELL, YA-UH!
- SHEEESH!
- I WOULDN'T HAVE MADE A VERY GOOD MONK OR COMPUTER EXPERT
- "WIT" HAD NONE
- *(Regarding Sal being peri-menopausal):* I USED TO WATCH *PERRY MASON,* SO I'M FAMILIAR WITH THAT
- YOU'RE NEVER GONNA GET ME TO ADMIT THAT—EVEN THOUGH THE EVIDENCE IS MOUNTIN' UP
- *(When Sal almost hit the neighbor's car):* FORTUNATELY, THE CLOSER YOU GET TO DEATH, THE MORE ENEMIES YOU CAN MAKE.
- I LOVE YOU LIKE A MILLION HAMBURGERS COOKED PRECISELY MY WAY, OVER A MILLION DIFFERENT DAYS

A tattoo he wanted us to get

SALLY'S
EC
NOTES

A line of mine Geo saved to put up front in his next book:

Sal: ONE FOOT IN FRONT OF THE OTHER— IT GETS YA GOIN'.

Sally, you upgraded me.

TO SAL

UNTIL NOW, YOU (7) WAS/WERE THE SMARTEST PERSON YOU/I KNEW.

I'M GOING TO ORDER MY SANDWICH NOW.

GEO TO SAL: YOU CAN make Benjamin Franklin look like A forgetful asshole

Things Geo was RIGHT about . . .

▶ YA KNOW, IF YOU'RE GONNA HAVE AN IRON, YOU MIGHT AS WELL HAVE AN IRONING BOARD.

▶ I'M SO SWEET, I'M WILLING TO FORGIVE YA EVEN WHEN YOU'VE DONE NOTHIN' WRONG.

Things Geo was WRONG about

KEEP SARAH JANE AWAY FROM "THE BASKET" Geo

I'LL BET YOU WON'T EVEN NOTICE THIS NOTE.

I'LL BET YOU WON'T EVEN NOTICE THIS NOTE.

I'LL BET YOU WON'T EVEN NOTICE THIS NOTE.

I'LL BET YOU WON'T EVEN NOTICE THIS NOTE.

YOU'RE
MY
EVERYTHING.

SALLY IS
MY BRASS RING,
A PRECIOUS PRIZE

BALLY'S
LAS VEGAS
25th Anniversary

Hi LADY LOVE —
THE BEST THING THAT'S
HAPPENED TO ME ALL YEAR—
BAR NOTHING — IS COMING
HOME TO YOU. NO FOOLIN',
COOKIE. YOU'RE MY PERMA-
NENT SWEET DREAM, AND,
ONCE AGAIN, IT'S COMING
TRUE.   LOVE ALWAYS GEO

What's nice about
an honest, bright
person is that
they're usually
fair.

TRUMP MARINA
HOTEL · CASINO
1-800-777-8477

Geo's
FAVORITE lines of Sal's:

▷ **MODERATION IS THE ROOT OF ALL EVIL.**

▷ **I HAD MORE SOY TODAY THAN THE COMBINED AVERAGE RESIDENTS OF IOWA.**

▷ **SHOPPING IS FINITE, WORK IS INFINITE.**

▷ **I ALWAYS TALK TO MYSELF. ALWAYS. THAT WAY I KNOW I'M IN GOOD COMPANY.**

▷ **TODAY IS THE FIRST DAY OF WHAT'S LEFT OF YOUR LIFE.**

Lines of Sal's that Geo writes down and saves:

"YA GOTTA GO WHERE THE CHANGE IS ... TO FIND CHANGE"
— WADE

SAL:
"You're Somethin'
+
Om Somethin,
else!"

WORK IS MERELY AN OPTION — AS LONG AS IT GETS DONE!
— WADE

SAL DECIDES TO EMBRACE P.M.S.

HUMOR ADDED TO COMEDY CANCEL EACH OTHER OUT. IT'S REDUNDANT.
— SALLY WADE

STO G
YOU MAKE AMBITION BORING.

This audience is as rigged as a Bellagio's nickel slot machine tryin' to pay off its floors

Sally said, "If you'd shut up, I could get some of my own writing done."

Spot's LEAST FAVORITE line of Geo's:

CALM DOWN — IT'S NOT A DUET

Geo's all-time FAVORITE:

SAL SEZ

JULY IS ALL-NAKED MONTH

SAL: Well, there you have it in a nutshell.
Geo: Or at least it's got a hard casing.

I THINK WE'RE QUITE A PEAR!

AND YOU'RE A PEACH.

love,
PRODUCE-MAN

CRANKY PANTS LOVES YOU !

GRUMPY SHORTS LOVES S.J. !

We finish each other's sentences.
Or at least he finishes mine . . .

TUES.
TARA

IF YOU AIN'T ONE ROMANTIC guy !!!

You bet yer sweet So + So.

YEAH, BABY!

SAL.
LOVE IS ALL WE NEED.

PLUS VITAMINS.

GEO

SALLY IS !
THE REST OF ME !

GEORGE IS:
THE BEST OF ME !

I MISS YOU too

I REALLY LOVE YOU too

Sal finished these sentences.

86

"hip" shouldn't mean what a lot of people think, it should mean ~~but~~ what a few hip people think.

You're not "impossible," you're just highly improbable.

Jupiter Jumbles

Geo creates Jupiter Jumbles for Sal to fill in.

The perfect cookie

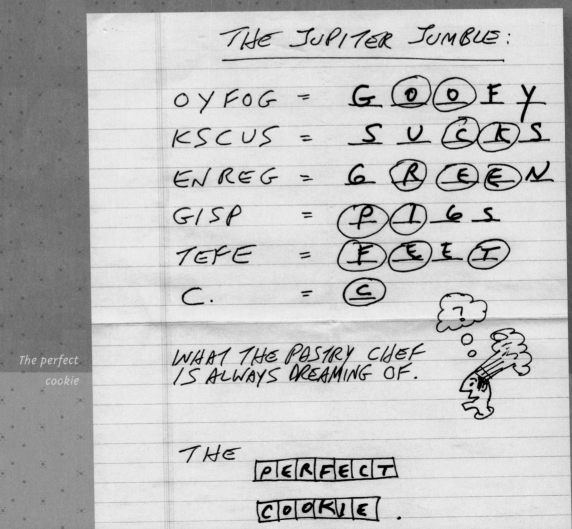

THE JUPITER JUMBLE:

OYFOG = G (O)(O) F Y

KSCUS = S U (C)(K) S

ENREG = G (R)(E)(E) N

GISP = (P)(I) G S

TEFE = (F)(E) E (I)

C. = (C)

WHAT THE PASTRY CHEF IS ALWAYS DREAMING OF.

THE

P E R F E C T

C O O K I E .

BIG BABY
A
GEOGIE
E
SALLY
O L
V Y
E O
    U

RIHGA ROYAL HOTEL
NEW YORK

Halloween 1998
Rm. 3410

To my lovely —

This place may be 54 stories, but it can't hold all my love. It's bursting out the windows; it's tumbling down the stairs — it's on every elevator. Get out of the way — Sally & George are in town. They're staying at the:

R eally   R esidence   H e's
I nto   O f   O n
H er   Y earning   T op
G orgeous   A nd   E njoying
A ss   L ust   L ove.

Love & special kisses
Your MANEUVERER
CITY BOY

151 WEST 54TH STREET, NEW YORK, NEW YORK 10019
(212) 307-5000 FAX (212) 765-6530 RESERVATIONS (800) 937-5454 TELEX (023) 210512 RIHGAR UR

The RIHGA Royal

H ave
A
R eally
L oving
E verlasting
M arriage

Harlem

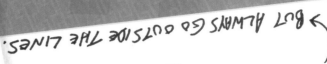

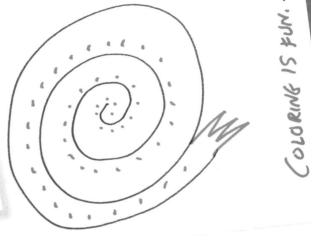

How loners become lovers . . . (by removing "I")

THE "SALGEO SPOT"

One night while making dinner at home, Geo, Sal, and Spot decide to open a restaurant on Jupiter called "The SalGeo Spot." The following is the menu we designed—a word-play on our names. It was one of those times when we couldn't stop laughing, and I couldn't grab a pen fast enough . . . maybe it was the wine Spot kept pouring.

The SalGeo Spot
MENU

CAESAR SAL-AD

IN-SAL-ATA — HOUSE SALAD

ANTI-PETS-SO

MUTT-ZARELLA MARINARA

BOW-LOGNESE WITH F-ARF-LAFEL

FART-L-AWFUL WITH BOW-LOGNESE

SPOT-GETTI AND MUTT-BALLS WITH PUPERONI

VEAL SAL-OPPINE DI GEO SITTIN' IN THE SAL-AD

CATCH OF THE DAY ON WEDNESDAY: SAL-MON

THURSDAY THROUGH TUESDAY: PET-ZA PIE WITH:

TO-MUTT-O SAUCE

PUP-PERONI

PAW-MESAN CHEESE

POOCH-INI MUSHROOMS

SAL-AMI

GREEN AND RED BELL PUP-PERS

DESSERTS:

TIRAMI-SAL

GEO-LOTTO

BI-SPOT-TI

We decide that our names are as rich with meaning as our food is rich with flavor.

Sally Wade
By Geo
Sweet
And
Lovely
Lady
You

Warm
And
Darling
Entity

George Carlin
By Spot Wade
Goes
Even
On
Rug
Gross
Everywhere

Cares
About
Really
Lame
Idiotic
Nouns

ACRONYMS

Sal's:

HMFWIC: Head motherfucker what's in charge *(pronounced "hemfwic")*

BFWOT: Big fuckin' waste of time *(pronounced "bufwot")*

Geo's:

AMDPWHATR: A mentally disturbed person who has access to the roof *(pronounced "amd-pa-watter")*

ITTHRHALTAF: I think the human race has a lot to answer for *(pronounced the way it's spelled)*

SWABWTTWTLYC:

(NOTE: private)

SWABWTTWTLYC

Sealed with a big wet tongue that wants to ~~lik~~ lick you cunt.

TRUMP MARINA
HOTEL · CASINO

Spot's:

SOLAFFB: Shit outta luck and falling far behind

EYE MIST
EWE TWO !

HEY COOKS—
BACK
INNA
MINNIT
GEO☆!

EYE
BEA
RYTE
BÄÄCK !

Jupiterian shorthand

91

HOW DO YOU TURN A PICTURE OF ALCATRAZ INTO A ROMANTIC CARD? ONLY CARLIN, THE CARD MASTER, CAN DO IT! PLEASE SEE INSIDE FOR DETAILS.

"A Picture of Alcatraz"

SOON I'LL BE OUTTA THIS CRUMMY JOINT!

Since childhood, I have used photography to capture moments that touched my soul. After working many jobs and saving money, I then backpacked numerous times all over the world. As my photography has developed, I have been surprised and thrilled to be invited to be a part of many art exhibitions in the US and Europe.

Here is one of my photos, signed, limited edition and suitable for matting and/or framing. As this card passes from hand to hand, I hope that it brings something to you as it has for me — and although we may never meet, I thank you for your interest in my work.

Marooner's Rock
P.O. Box 903
Beverly Hills
CA   90213
© S. Darling

Suzanne Darling

MAY
062498
L.M
23 24 25 21 22

Counting the days until Geo sees Sal.

You are the machine gun in the guard tower of my heart.

"Psssst! WANT TO BUY SOME FREECHY LICENSE PLATES?"

PRISONER # 062493

HEY GIRLY GIRL!
When on the road, I am not free — I am locked in the prison of separation and my every cell longs to escape this solitary life. I guard against depression and I'm wardin' off the blues. Soon I'll be paroled and remanded to the half-way house of your love. As a man of conviction, I appeal to you to help me end these sentences. Thanks — A LIFER, JUPITER GEORGE

"Cookies and Cakes"
(Sal's nickname is Cookie, Geo's is Cakes)

I'M
FRESH
OUT OF
PUNS.

BUT NOT LOVE

Imported By S...
www.vint...

* ②

- NOT TO MENTION A COUPLE OF STEP-DONUTS, THROUGH A PREVIOUS BAKERY. I'D ALSO LIKE TO VISIT WITH MY GREAT-GRAND TART. GET SOME DOUGH, AND WE'LL FLY Y-EAST TOWARD THE RISING SUN AND GET HALF-BAKED ON FRENCH WINE, AFTER COUNTLESS TOASTS. THEN I'LL PUT MY LOAF IN YOUR OVEN.

SIGNED - THE WELL-BREAD MR. C. ARLIN

IT TAKES SOME CRUST TO WRITE A CRUMBY CARD LIKE THIS.

START HERE   START HERE   START HERE

① FROM GOOFOIS TO GOOFOISE —

TAKE ME HERE, SAL (COVER), ON ONE OF OUR TRIPS IN 2002. IT'S ABOUT TIME A COOKIE AND A CAKE WENT TO AN ACTUAL BAKERY AND VISITED THEIR RELATIVES. I'VE GOT A CROISSANT-IN-LAW I HAVEN'T SEEN IN YEARS. ☼

GOOFY TEXT MESSAGE

GEO: Nice, fast typin', Cooks.

SAL: Thanks, Cake. Strawwwwwberry shortcake. That's what you are. Hi, hi. Come in, please.

GEO: When do I get to talk?

SAL: Oh, pleaaaaaaaseeeeee. Boy are you goofy. Mister Two Fingers—let's get goin'.

GEO: I'm gonna sign out, legs. I got a life to live.

SAL: Ha, ha. I'll miss you.

GEO: Fongool!

SAL: What's that? Some Korean dish? Raw cock?

GEO: Naah, it means "fuck you" in Italian.

SAL: You sure it's not "raw cock"?

GEO: If you insist.

SAL: Yum!

GEO: Jesus!!!!

SAL: Over & out. More tomorrow.

GEO: You ain't kiddin'. "More tomorrow."

A FEW E-MAILS FROM GEO TO SAL

☐ Save Outgoing Message   **Send**   **Save Draft**   **Cancel**

Good morning, sweetness;

I want to say again how wonderful it is to be with you --in life, in love. You are so very special and gifted and giving; you bring such pleasure and happiness to me; our life together has such richness and substance and pleasure ——it all seems like a dream. After the lucky life I've had, I'll never understand how I deserve all this. Thank you for your love. And thanks to Spot for knowing a good guy when he sees one.

About my sweet Sara-Jane:
Here is something you know but have to re-learn every day:

You have to keep giving yourself the benefit of the doubt

☐ Save Outgoing Message   **Send**   **Save Draft**   **Cancel**

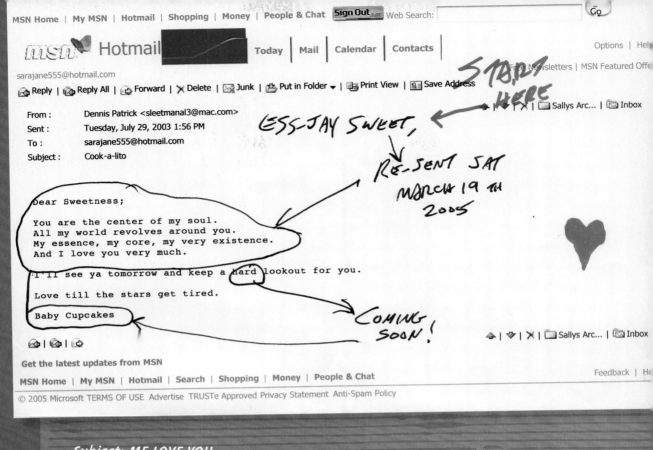

Subject: ME LOVE YOU
Date: January 1, 2007, 12:02 p.m.

GEO: You're my peachy-rose, the pearlie-girlie of the Ozarks and all other
mountain ranges everywhere, including the moon, which is where I will take
you on a vacation on our way to Jupiter, which is where we live.
Pack yer bags, Toots.
I love you

I e-mail him back:

Subject: Re: ME LOVE YOU
Date: January 1, 2007 12:37 p.m. PST

SAL: My bags are packed. When are we leaving?
Toots

I'm still waiting to hear back . . .

SPOT—
   O MI GOD
HERE THEY COME AGAIN!
FROM JUPITER.
TELL YOUR LADY MY GUY
   LOVES HER.
                    STAIN

CHAPTER 8

Spot & Geo

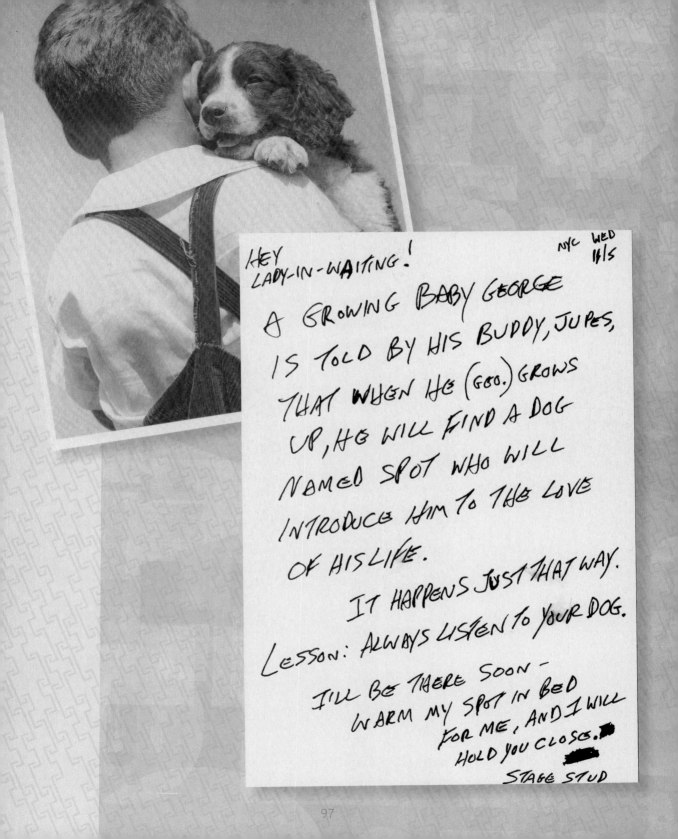

Spot Wade's
"Bone" Mots
All Spot's writing is channeled by Sal

One can become complacent due to **the repetitiveness of chicken.**

Make my last meal everything out of the prison vending machine. **Just empty it.**

A bone of contention: Two dogs wantin' the same bone.

Politics is useless if you're in the minority.

I've got a **rare chewing disorder.** It's called "Bone-lemia."

A Master Cleanse: A dog giving its owner a bath.

I got a bath today, which gave me ODD—**Odor Deficiency Disorder.**

I told the vet who fondled my tags to stay away from my **bling-bling.**

As a dog thinketh, so he is.

Walking: an exercise in **preventative farting.**

New word: Instead of "Palm-erhyperhydrosis," **"Paw-merhyperhydrosis"**—those who suffer from sweaty paws.

Brainer

George Carlin

No-Brainer

BRAINER/NO-BRAINER

Spot claims that Geo has plastic surgery in order to look like him and steal his trademark expression. He even threatens to sue Geo for identity theft and is willing to take it all the way to the supreme court. Until finally, they find they share a mutual goal—drinking. Just a little bit, not much! A couple of beers in the afternoon. They both agree—in fact, Spot says Geo told him—"It's not only good for your heart, it helps you take a nap."

SPOT: *Can you hand me that beer on the second shelf, left-hand side, Mr. Carlin?*

GEO: *Whatcha want, little buddy, is Purple Label Ronrico 151-proof rum, 75 percent alcohol. It gets ya drunk real fast.*

SPOT: *Then hand me that instead, please. I haven't got all day.*

99

**Spot Wade's
Drunken Redundancies**
Dog Droppings
As dictated to Geo and channeled by Sal

For Jean!

WHEN WILL
JESUS
BRING THE
PORK CHOPS?

ANSWER:
When Spot gets ready
to order them!!
Best to you always—
George Carlin

"..Dog's Droppings"..

DRUNKEN DOG
SPOT'S &
WADE'S REDUNDACIES for GEORGE
CARLINS NEXT
BOOK SIT DOWN
DOO DOO
DUMB CAT   CRABBY OWNER
BAD BEHAVIOR   GREAT-LOOKIN DOG   FAT ASS
BUNNY RABBIT   CHILD OFFENDER
TERRIBLE BATH HOLY SHIT
RATHOLE GARAGE   DUMB IDEA
CRAPPY SEWER
                        YOU STINK
FAT ASS
DUMB IDEA
UNRULY CHILDREN

STUPID PEOPLE
UNHEALTHFUL HABITS
GO AWAY!   — Spot

"Bone" Mots
By Spot & Geo

Imagine meeting your maker and finding out it's Mattel?

SPOT: You know why I don't like the mailman?

GEO: No, why?

SPOT: Because he's always goin' postal on ya.

GEO: *(on a walk with Spot):* Try and keep up, will ya?

SPOT: What do ya mean? Intellectually? I've lapped ya.

GEO: This is Beethoven, baby!

SPOT: *(covering his ears):* You can tell he was deaf.

Geo's language lesson for Spot

❶ Who is John Jacob Astor?

A. *A wealthy merchant and fur trader, whose money influenced public policy.*

B. *The son of a butcher, who made the American fur trade pre-eminent.*

✓ C. *The first major drug dealer, who smuggled opium.*

❷ Why does the U.S.A. spend $100 billion a year on getting high?

A. *Because they need it. If it wasn't for alcohol, half of you never would have been conceived.*

B. *The problem goes back to Descartes: If "I am," then "I am here . . ." and all else is "out there," then I am separated permanently from "all else." And it takes too much effort to see that we are not separated—that it is all "one." But most dogs are not capable of making that effort—hence the "anxiety of separation," and our need to relieve the pain, and change the way we feel.*

✓ C. *Who cares, as long as the automatic coffeemaker is set so you'll get a nice lift in the morning?*

❸ Define "lottery."

A. *Odds that are overwhelming.*

✗ B. *I don't know about you, but I'm willing to take a chance and leave my owners.*

C. *How we voluntarily get more money from the people and give it to the government.*

✓ *Wrong: answer C is correct.*

ME + SPOT THINK YOU'RE PRETTY COOL.

Spot's language lesson for Geo

1 What is the news media?

   A. *Your friend—treat them with respect and they can make you rich and famous.*

     B. *Always something new. Isn't that why they call it news?*

  ✔ C. *A cesspool of corrupt and intimidated patsies, who regularly and routinely accept government handouts and pat answers without doing the hard work of checking facts and digging deeper. (George adds, "So that big asshole they're reaming out is yours!")*

SPOT: WRONG! Don't editorialize!

2 We're looking good longer because of:

A. *Fresher water*

B. *Organic food*

✔ C. *12 million dollars spent on cosmetic surgeries last year alone.*

3 Shopping carts these days:

   A. *Have a system that locks the wheels if you try to take it off the premises.*

   B. *Turn in circles, no matter how you steer.*

   C. *Have electronic or digital equipment so the store can track their whereabouts.*

  ✔ D. *Who cares?*

   E. *All of the above.*

Spot: WRONG! E

Score totals:
THE LOSER: George: 1½
THE WINNER: Spot: 2
Spot wins!

E-MAILS BETWEEN SPOT AND GEO

When Spot sees how well Geo orders dinner and handles the press, he hires him to be his P.A., rep, and editor for his upcoming book, *From the Desk of Spot Wade,* and they begin to exchange e-mails regularly.

BOY OH BOY

ARF ARF!

KEEP IT UP, SPOTTIE BOY. YOU'RE DOIN' GREAT!

YOUR STEP-DAD + PAL GEO

- AND GIVE YOUR MOM A BIG WET KISS FOR ME.

On Nov 29, 2005, at 3:39 PM, Spot Wade wrote:

dear mister carlin,

i've been thinking about what to get my loyal, most trusted employees for x-mas and wondered if you might like one of these battery-operated heated fleece vests. if so, send me the moula and i'll go pick one up for you at my earliest convenience.

THANK YOU FOR YOUR KIND AND THOUGHTFUL OFFER, MR. SPOT. ALTHOUGH IT'S NOT QUITE MY STYLE OF THING, I NOTICE IT'S A PERFECT SIZE FOR HEATING A MID-SIZED DOG IN A COLD, CHICKEN-LESS GARAGE. ANY CONNECTION HERE? HOPE I'M NOT BEIN' TOO CYNICAL. YOU KNOW HOW MUCH I LOVE YOU, GUY.

YOUR FAITHFUL SERVANT,

MR. CARLIN

GEO WRITES TO SPOT

Monsieur Spotois,

Arf, arf, arf, arf! Woof! Woof! Gr-r-r-r-r-r! Grrrr! Ruff! Arrrrghh! And furthermore, bow-wow-wow, ya little prick. How do ya like that?
Your Step-dad

SPOT WRITES TO GEO

Dear father who are in Vegas,

Arf, arf, arf? And grrr . . . And ruff translates into many things in dog language depending on attitude and inflection—so my question to you is this: Are you sure you know what you're talking about? If not, I suggest you cut the crap and write in plain English. If you're constipated, I'll send ya some Pepto-Bismol.
As always,
Nose-scraped-today-to-see-if-I-got-mites-and-I-don't,
Spot the Great

SPOT WRITES AGAIN

Dear Bucky,

It has come to my attention that you have not responded to me as quickly as I'd hoped. Is this some type of hoax—or are you having trouble on the toilet again?

All my best,

Spot Wade, Bucky #2

Subject: **Re: HEY SPOT!**
Date: April 30, 2006 3:19:37 PM PDT
To: Spot Wade <spotwade@comcast.net>
Cc: Dennis Patrick <sleetmanal3@mac.com>

DON'T BRING GOD INTO IT.

On Apr 30, 2006, at 3:05 PM, Spot Wade wrote:

> GOD PUNISHES THOSE WHO MAKE FUN OF TALKING DOGS.
> On Apr 30, 2006, at 2:55 PM, Dennis Patrick wrote:
>
> > HEY SPOT, YOU GETTIN' ANY MAIL LATELY?
> >
> > EDITOR
> >
> > <TalkingDogs.wmv>

See Spot run!

DIRTY, MISOGYNISTIC JOKES THAT SPOT STEALS OFF THE INTERNET, THEN TRADES TO GEO FOR PIECES OF TURKEY SANDWICHES

Spot: How do you get a dog to stop humping your leg?

Geo: How?

Spot: Pick him up and suck his dick.

Spot: How do you keep a jackass in suspense?

Geo: How?

Spot: I'll let you know tomorrow!

Spot: Have you heard about the earthquake in Mexico?

Geo: No.

Spot: One hundred million dollars in improvements.

Geo: That's not nice.

Spot: A word about being nice: It's not consistent with the integrity of my character.

MORNING DRAMA
By Geo, for Spot

Rockford, Illinois.

The morning outlook seemed positive, but distant clouds suggested Sunday held other possibilities. As eyes opened and muscles lengthened into daytime form—and with a quick but powerful morning fart now out of the way and ringing off the hotel walls—a Diet Coke seemed a logical and desirable next step.

Just a few steps down the hall stood the mighty and majestic Coke machine—bright, cheerful, and eager to please its guests in need of a chemical stimulus . . . but only at a price. One dollar, please. Bills preferred, change accepted, but definitely no checks or credit cards.

His wallet offered little comfort: credit cards aplenty, a lone blank check, and a number of soft green bills, none of which, however, bore the magic words—the keys to a day's good start—"one dollar." The change situation was hardly better: two quarters, three dimes, and a nickel; eighty-five cents, fifteen short of the magic world of caffeine. Not a good situation, especially as the hotel desk was a long way off in this sprawling suburban hotel-convention-theater complex—a journey a newly awakened comedian, whose hair resembled that of Dr. Zorba, did not wish to take. Not with all those wretched soccer families mingling and milling about.

And then it happened: distant trumpets just beyond the ridge! The cavalry! There, peeking over the edge of one of the slots of his wallet, obscuring the credit cards now rendered impotent by the big, friendly machine, were several hand-printed block letters screaming at him in red ink: S-P-O-T! Fuckin' SPOT! The dollar bill Spot had given him recently as a loving gift was now winking at him knowingly, saying, "I love you, Daddy; here's your Coca-Cola!" Thank you, oh Spotster. Thank you, thank you, thank you. And fuck Lassie!

HOW MY LIFE IRREVOCABLY CHANGED OVERNIGHT, DUE TO AN ALIEN ABDUCTION

By Spot

Spot in the ER

To put it bluntly, first my owner and my personal assistant and rep, George Carlin, dumped me at the vet—where they say they are going to "fix me," when I don't know what's wrong. Then I black out and wake up back in my own garage, which is where some idiots leave me overnight, to go out and have dinner and wine without me. YOU GUYS!!!!!!

At approximately three a.m., I was visited by an alien spacecraft—with extraterrestrial beings that then conducted an experiment on me, at least that's what I think, because when I woke up around four, four-thirty, my "manhood" was missing.

I'm thinking they must've taken me to Mars or Venus (sometime between three and four-thirty), then tampered with my "parts related to reproduction"—by cuttin' 'em off—and examining them under a microscope to see what makes me so smart compared to George Carlin! In my humble opinion, why else would they need balls from a guy like me, I ask you? Huh? Otherwise, the whole thing makes no sense whatsoever.

Spot's Facebook girlfriend, Molly, who lives in London.
P.S. Don't tell Molly about the alien abduction!!!!!!!!!!!!!!!!!!

Spot's best Facebook friend, and pub-hopping partner from London, the all-knowing Midder Mac Shaw, who suffered a similar experience. This is where the expression "hang dog" originated.

Report Card

DISCIPLINE Mothering

NAME SALLY THE OWNER LADY

REQUIREMENTS Subject Area	Grade	Plus/Minus	Comment	ELECTIVES Subject Area	Grade	Plus/Minus	Comment
Maternal Nurturance	A		1	Initial Father Selection	A		1
Lesson Teaching	A F		8	Eye Twinkling	A A		1
Example Setting	C		2	Financial Assistance	A A		1
Transmission of Ethics ?	C			Youthful Joie de Vivre	A A		1
Pride in Offspring	C A A		1	Spree Shopping	A+ ++		
Patience (i.e. Saints)	A A		1	Nagging	A N	—	
Supportiveness	A		1	Blind Boosterism	N A		1
Self-Sacrifice	B		2	Needless Worrying	F A		4
Making It All Better	A A		1	Provision of Gossip	A A		1
Unconditional Love	A		1	Acceptance	A A		1

Grading:
A = Excellent
B = Above Average
C = Average
D = Below Average
F = Failure
N = Incomplete or

Key to
1. Well
2. Show
3. Contr
4. Work
5. Follow
6. ....

Sally the Owner Lady's report card, as dictated by Spot to his P.A., George Carlin

A note Spot thinks Geo wrote to him

Different spot, Spot

Hi

Hi

Hi Hi

Blech!

HEY GIRL!

WISH I WAS LYIN'
IN MY USUAL SPOT;
I'D REACH OVER
AND START SOMETHING.

YOU A SEXY THING.

I'LL BE BACK.
KEEP IT WARM.

NITEY-NITE   GEO

CHOCOLATE

you can never have too much!.........

CHAPTER 9

Time for Romance

I MISS YOU EVERY SECOND OF EVERY DAY, SALLY.

IT'S LIKE LIVING HALF A LIFE. LESS! IT'S LIKE A THIRD OF A LIFE. I CAN'T WAIT TO BE IN YOUR ARMS AGAIN AND TO SEE YOUR PRETTY EYES. I LOVE YOU.

WOW — THERE GOES LIL SARA JANE FLYIN' OFF WITH HER SWEET CUPCAKE. WONDER WHERE THEY'RE GOIN'? PROBABLY TO JUPITER, THEIR HOME PLANET. AND WHERE'D SHE GET THAT TERIFIC HAT? A STAR HAT! WOW. JUST WHAT SHE DESERVES.

AND THOSE STRIPED PANTY-HOSE! WHAT A TREND-SETTER THIS GAL IS. THE UNIVERSE WILL NEVER BE THE SAME.

LOVE YOU LOTS OF BUNCHES
THE ORIGINAL BABY CHOCOLATE CUPCAKE

Our love was **instant**.

Geo had a huge, huge heart. It happened spontaneously—falling in love—it was love and stars and Jupiter and the moon, and bridges, and . . . I just soaked it in.

He was actually more of a poet than a comedian. Every night, Geo—adlibbing a poem of how much he loved me—spun out a web of protection, making me feel safe with his words, with his vocabulary.

I Love You More Than . . .

- **SAL, I LOVE YOU MORE THAN ALL THE STUFF EVERYWHERE, TIMES ITSELF EVERY SECOND INTO INFINITY. SO THERE!**

- If you took all the sick people at Cedars and made them well instantly—the way they would feel combined is not equal to as much as I feel on my worst day with you.

- I love you more than all the feathers in all the pillows in the world.

- All the flowers that ever lived, times all the stars that ever shined, are not as beautiful as my honey, Sal, the Pearl of the Ozarks.

Geo proves his love through **mathematics**

YOU TAKE ALL THE RAINDROPS THAT HAVE FALLEN THIS YEAR IN CALIFORNIA,

AND YOU ADD ALL THE SNOWFLAKES THAT HAVE FALLEN THIS YEAR IN CALIFORNIA AT HIGHER ALTITUDES,

AND YOU MULTIPLY THAT BY ALL THE CARS SARA JANE HAS LOOKED AT THIS YEAR,

AND YOU ADD ALL THE ASSHOLES THAT WORK FOR BMW WORLDWIDE,

AND YOU MULTIPLY BY ALL THE ENGINES IN THE WORLD THAT HAVE EVER SURGED,

AND YOU ADD ALL THE PENNIES THAT JACK HAS MANAGED NOT TO SPEND OVER THE YEARS,

AND YOU ADD ALL THE TIMES GOOFY DIDN'T HEEL,

AND YOU TAKE THAT NUMBER AND MULTIPLY IT BY ITSELF AND DIVIDE BY ONE.

THEN YOU ADD 55.

AND YOU HAVE JUST THE BEGINNINGS OF A SMALL HINT, LEADING TO THE MILDEST POSSIBLE SUGGESTION OF THE AMOUNT OF LOVE, ADMIRATION, APPRECIATION AND RESPECT I HAVE FOR YOU, MY SWEET SALLY. I DEARLY ADORE YOU. AND 'TWILL EVER BE THUS.

YOUR GUY,

JUMPIN' JUPITER GEORGE
(KING AND RESIDENT SWEETHEART)

SALLYBURGER,

If you took all the number of sub-atomic part-icles in the universe and multiplied that number times itself THAT MANY TIMES, and then added the total number of MICRO-SECONDS since the beginning of time, times itself; and then added 803 — you would still have only the barest fraction OF A BILLION-BILLIONTH PER CENT of the amount of love I HAVE FOR YOU.

Love,
Your candle partner,
the romantic Mr. Carlin,
your eternal flame.

MB + SAL

Am gonna love you more in the next minute than all the people in all the history of the world have ever loved each other.

Take all the MOLECULES of all the water — in all the OCEANS, LAKES, RIVERS, FOG, MIST + VAPOR in the History of the UNIV + MULT X ITSELF + then take all the PHOTONS of ALL THE BEAMS of ALL THE LIGHT from all the STARS in all the GAL that ever existed and MULT it X itself + that is only a small portion of how much I love you, Sally Wade.

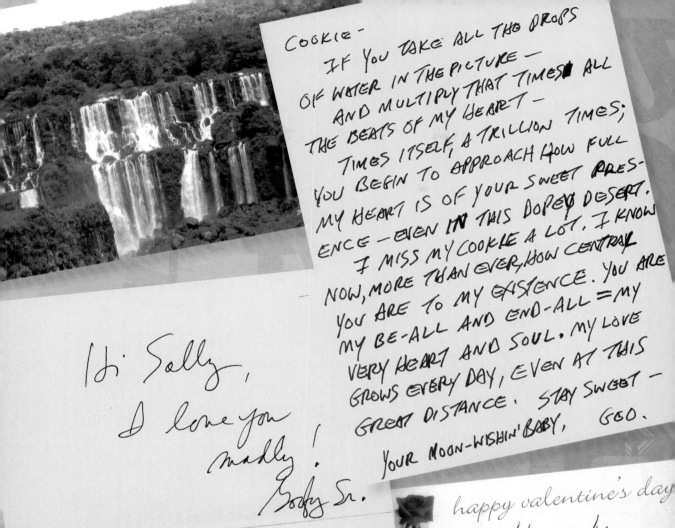

Cookie—

IF YOU TAKE ALL THE DROPS OF WATER IN THE PICTURE— AND MULTIPLY THAT TIMES THE BEATS OF MY HEART— TIMES ITSELF, A TRILLION TIMES, YOU BEGIN TO APPROACH HOW FULL MY HEART IS OF YOUR SWEET PRESENCE—EVEN IN THIS DOPEY DESERT.

I MISS MY COOKIE A LOT. I KNOW NOW, MORE THAN EVER, HOW CENTRAL YOU ARE TO MY EXISTENCE. YOU ARE MY BE-ALL AND END-ALL = MY VERY HEART AND SOUL. MY LOVE GROWS EVERY DAY, EVEN AT THIS GREAT DISTANCE. STAY SWEET—

YOUR MOON-WISHIN' BABY,   GEO.

Hi Sally,
I love you
madly!
Booby Sr.

IF YOU MULTIPLY ALL THE LEAVES THAT EVER SPROUTED, AND ALL BLADES OF GRASS THAT EVER PEEPED UP THEIR LITTLE HEADS, TIMES ALL THE BIRDS THAT EVER SANG A PRETTY SONG, YOU BEGIN TO APPROACH THE LEVEL OF MY DEEP LOVE FOR YOU. I MISS YOU GREATLY.

KEEP ME IN YOUR HEART—

YOU LIVE IN MINE.

happy valentine's day

To the only Valentine I've ever had.
Love, Carlin
George

Favorite **romantic** lines **by Geo**

"Within fifty trillion years, what are the odds of Geo and Sal coming together?"
—GEORGE CARLIN

I EVEN LOVE YOU FOR YOUR MIND!

(AND YOU THOUGHT I JUST WANTED YOUR BODY.)

HAPPY VALENTINE'S DAY

I'LL LOVE YOU NORE EVERY DAY FOR A BILLION LIFETIMES.

YORE GUY — GEO

I CAN'T TELL YOU HOW GOOD IT FEELS TO BE WITH YOU ON THIS VALENTINE'S DAY. IT ALL SEEMS SO PRE-ORDAINED AND SO PERFECT. OUR LOVE IS THE MOST WONDERFUL THING I HAVE EVER EXPERIENCED. I TREASURE YOU BEYOND EXISTENCE ITSELF. PLEASE STAY IN MY ARMS FOREVER — YOU ALREADY HAVE A PERMANENT SPOT IN MY HEART.
SEÑOR CUPCAKE

**TO SAL
MY ETERNAL VALENTINE
I LOVE YOU
GEO**

Hey, girl —
It just keeps getting better & better & better, doesn't it? What a lucky couple we are to find our way through 5,999,999,998 other people and happen upon each other. I'll never get over it. And I'll _never_ stop loving the loving.
Your absolutely the finest of the fine and the mostest of the most. — GEORGIE BOY

IF YOU WERE ANY PRETTIER, THE SUN WOULD BE EMBARRASSED THAT YOU OUT-SHONE HIM.

I'M SO IN LOVE WITH YOU I COULD BURST — BUT I PROMISE TO CLEAN UP THE MESS.

"We almost feel like it's a betrayal now to do our own work."
—SALLY WADE

SCHMERKENFESTER

KRELDENMACHER

FLOYDENSTEIGEN

wow!

Subject :   valentine love

Sweet Sara, My Dream;
I have never been so in love, and I've never had a better Valentine that you.
You are the key to my happiness, and I love you with all my heart.
Forever Yours in the Bubble,
George

As Geo was enjoying a handful of walnuts: "I have never liked any kind of nuts in my life—except peanuts and cashews—until I met you."
~GEORGE CARLIN

S—

YOU PUT YOURSELF RIGHT WHERE YOU WERE NEEDED — BETWEEN ME & MY MINDLESS MIND. YOU BROKE UP THE PATTERN.

BALLY'S
LAS VEGAS
25th Anniversary

← YOU SAVED MY ASS/ G

HERE'S HOW MUCH I LOVE YOU:

○ ← THE UNIVERSE

SEE YA SOON —

SWEET ROSE OF MY HEART — I'M ONLY ABOUT 20% OF MYSELF WITHOUT YOU — I'LL BE HOME SOON TO CLAIM THE OTHER 80%. I CAN'T TELL YA HOW MUCH I MISS YA. I LOVE YOU WITH ALL MY HEART. AND I ALWAYS WILL. LOVE LOVE LOVE

LADY,
I want you to know...
I'm still courting you.

KELLA

THE JUPITER TWINS

G. TO S.

You could kill 6 children tomorrow, and I would still be firmly in your corner.

YOU'RE LIKE NOTHING
~~EVER~~
~~I~~ COULD HAVE ~~EVER~~
~~EX~~ EXPECTED, AND YOU'RE
EVERYTHING I THOUGHT
YOU WOULD BE.

MY ~~PEARL~~

RR
RIHGA ROYAL HOTEL
NEW YORK

"You're the good part
of a ~~dig~~ disgusting
oyster."

— CARLIN

YOU'VE TURNED ME
INTO A COMPLETELY
SANE MANIAC!

Geo's romantic foreplay lines to Sal

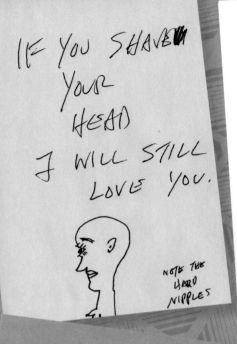

- Ya know, there's no law that we can't have sex just because you're tired and in pain.
- I don't care how ya look. Ya look horrible? That's fine.
- Hey, baby! The moon is doin' somethin' you don't do—holdin' water!
- I'll be upstairs before long for a mutual equipment inspection. I'll pat yer butt.
- You got a TV in your kitchen? You're a woman worth stayin' with!
- Man, it's been so long since I've had a shower, there is not enough hot water in this house for me to get scrubbed up properly!
- The day you're not sexy to me is the day the moon jumps up and down and sings "That's Amore."

Sal's romantic foreplay lines to Geo

- **You send me to outer space and bring me down to Earth at the same time.**

- **Welcome home, Geo! Don't forget the World Series today! Red Sox and Cardinals! First time since 1967! Love, *le moi!* I got ya TiVoed – comin' and goin', so ya won't miss a thing!**

- **P.S. There's also a piece of carrot cake on the top shelf of the fridge. Be forewarned! It has real sugar!**

- **Be back in time to love you more than I already do!**

Geo wasn't anti sexist jokes—he was anti *simpleminded* sexist jokes. (Unless we were under the covers with a flashlight playing tent with the sheets, of course.) If anybody assumes George was a chauvinist, they would be wrong. If anything—like me—he was anti straight, white, racist males, and felt they have a lot to answer for. And if I'm mad at Geo for anything, it's for leaving me in a chauvinistic world without him. He did not like "white men," and their "commerce," and felt that only men who hadn't dealt with their feminine side still engaged in such an old, arrogant male custom.

Sally
Teach me
to be
a perfect man.
George

TRUMP MARINA
HOTEL · CASINO
1-800-777-8477

Geo would snub men who made chauvinistic comments to him in front of me, thinking he'd find them funny. He'd tell them to **"shut the fuccck up."** Then he'd put his arm around me, and we'd turn and walk away. **"That'll teach 'em,"** he'd say, making sure they overheard.

If we had a penny for every time some asshole came up to us and said something off-color—just because he was George Carlin—we could fill the fountain at the New York–New York casino in Vegas. It pissed him off that they missed the point entirely, that they didn't get the big picture. Which is the one Geo draws himself into . . .

Annual Meeting of Single, Straight, Emotionally-Stable, Financially-Secure, Intelligent Men Looking for a Long-Term Commitment

Need I say more?

It's me!
Your lover

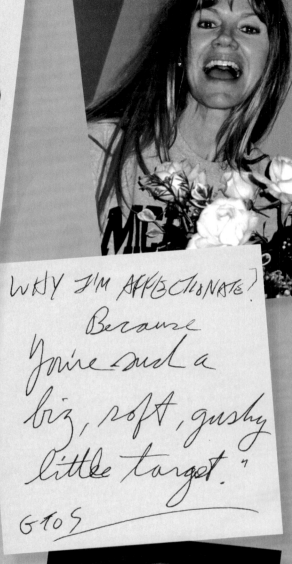

He'd use my name in every sentence he could.

He'd say, "Hello, this is George Carlin. Sally and I would like a table for two." As if anybody knew who Sally was.

When I'd land in New York, the limo driver would come up to me and say, "Are you Sally?"

"Yes."

Instead of saying, "The car is this way," the driver, usually the amazing Ira Berlowitz, who knows every shortcut from Manhattan to Atlantic City, would read from a note, saying, "George said to tell you he loves you madly and deeply." When I'd get to the hotel, the concierge would say something similar. And so would the card with the flowers that were waiting. A trail of breadcrumbs left by Geo.

Geo sends Sal flowers at the RIHGA
Royal Hotel in New York . . .

(LOVELY, NOT LONELY)

Hey Lonely —

Roses for the really
regal and Royal Rihga
Royal recipient of
romantic rhapsodies
righteously rendered
by your eternal lover
(RAN out of R's)

CARTE PO

Address

My dearest Sally —

Hi. I love you with all my heart.
You have captured me with your
charm, wit, beauty, grace and character. The fact that you love me
as much as you do is the greatest thrill I have ever known.

Love RELENTLESSLY, YOUR GUY

Geo and Sal,
in the year 2088

CHAPTER 10

Marriage of the King
& Queen of Jupiter

JUPITER

BIG RED
SPOT

MAGNETIC
FORCE
FIELD

SHUTTLE
SHIP
FROM
JOPLIN

EARTH

READ STORY FIRST

A STARTLING GLIMPSE INTO THE FUTURE SHOWS SAL & GEO CELEBRATING THE 90TH ANNIVERSARY OF THEIR LUNCH AT IL FORNAIO — IN 2088 — AT THEIR LONGTIME HOME IN KEY WEST, MISSOURI. THE GREAT EARTHQUAKE OF 2021 HAD MOVED FLORIDA INTO THE OZARKS. FRED & ETHEL OPENED A JUICE BAR IN BUCK CREEK, AND LENORE AND JIM STARTED A DEEP-SEA FISHING-CHARTER SERVICE, HIRING DANNY AS A GUIDE. SAL & GEO WERE THE FIRST TWO EARTH TOURISTS TO VISIT JUPITER ON THE TRANS-SOLAR SHUTTLE IN 2033. THEY DIDN'T NEED SUCH MUNDANE MEANS FOR REACHING THEIR HOME PLANET, BEING KING AND QUEEN, AND HAVING SUPER-EARTHLY ABILITIES TO TRANS-TELEPORT THEMSELVES ANYWHERE IN THE UNIVERSE, BUT THEY DID IT IN ORDER TO CHECK OUT THE SHUTTLE AND TO EVALUATE THE MEANS BY WHICH FAT, UGLY TOURISTS FROM MISSOURI AND ARKANSAS WOULD BE FOULING THEIR PRECIOUS, GASEOUS HOME. THEY DECIDED TO CREATE A MAGNETIC FORCE FIELD THAT WOULD REPEL THE SHUTTLE SHIPS AND DIVERT THEM INTO ETERNAL ORBITS AROUND ONE OF THE DEAD MOONS OF URANUS.
END OF STORY   I LOVE YOU

Just so you know . . . Fred and Ethel had a juice bar in Key West, and Danny was
the fishing guide. Lenore and Jim are Sal's mother and brother.

By the way, how's this for a marriage proposal?

Did anyone else get one like this? Geo was waiting for Sal at the bar of Wolfgang Puck's Chinois restaurant on Main Street. He was going to eat catfish for the very first time— must-have catfish that only Chinois has. And while he's waiting, he writes this:

SAL'S MARRIAGE PROPOSAL FROM GEO

Gonna eat catfish. Can't believe it! Catfish!
I must really love Sally.
Well, she loves me — along with Spot and anything chocolate after 6 o'clock.
What a woman!
Am so ~~Ba~~ in love.
So, so in love.

Please marry me, Sally.

Three things can be deduced from this note . . .

1. He didn't really know if he liked catfish or not.

2. He puts himself right in there along with "Spot and anything chocolate after six o'clock," which is *the* place to be.

3. It's a George Carlin marriage proposal. Nobody else could have followed it up with this illustration to add to its directness quite like Geo

Sal is so afraid of getting married again, that she says, "Geo'gie? Do you know what a long way vows have come since 'love, honor, and obey'? Now, when people get married, they gotta support each other's freakin' dreams, as well as retain their own identity! Hell, I'd rather hold water than do all that! Why don't we just eat dessert instead?"

Geo reassures me that on Jupiter, supporting each other's dreams and retaining an individual identity are just *excess baggage*. "Make-work," he says, convincingly.

He was fairly insistent that we have some sort of ceremony though.

So we were married on Jupiter.

We flew all the way there in our spacemobile, with Spot at the control panels, and Geo and I sitting outside on the wing in lounge chairs—*drinking piña coladas*—on the lookout for meteorites and other stray space particles that might cause a cosmic explosion equal to our love. Fortunately, I've always been a proponent of high magic, so *using mental telepathy* to ward off collisions was fairly easy, and there were no debris dents in the Jupiterian spaceship to repair once we returned.

It didn't take that long, *if* you're not COUNTING CENTURIES—which we made up for on the way back, of course, with age reversal. In fact, nobody even noticed we were gone (that's the beauty of time travel). I think we were absent from Earth five, ten minutes tops. The same length of time it takes me to write this paragraph, oddly enough.

The Red Devil Dog from Jupiter, who solemnizes the marriage between Jupiter Geo & Jupiter Sal

WE WERE MARRIED BY WILLIAM WEGMAN'S FAMOUS RED DEVIL DOG ON JUPITER . . .
As opposed to by some fiduciary picking his nose at City Hall here on Earth. We wanted no part of the government on this planet, *or that fiduciary,* sticking his nose into our marital affairs.

Hi Sally — You sweet slut! Spot claims to know the dog on the cover — claims he met him on the beach at Ensenada. They smoked pot together. Spot explained our love and passion and our sexual behavior quite graphically — the other dog fainted, but agreed to perform the ceremony. Your devoted SLAVE

DEAR READER—ESPECIALLY LOVELY SALLY—
THE DOGS OF JUPITER ARE A
STRANGE LOT. THE DOG PICTURED
IS A "STANDING RED DEVIL DOG."
THEY ARE THE ONLY CREATURES
ON THE PLANET EMPOWERED TO
PERFORM WEDDING CEREMONIES.
ALL IS NORMAL, TILL THE END,
WHEN THE DOG HUNCHES THE
GROOM'S LEG. HE IS EAGERLY
_{THIS DOG, GOOFY,}
ANTICIPATING GEORGE'S SHAPELY
LEFT CALF AS GEORGE AND SAL-
LY'S JUPITERIAN FUSION CERE-
MONY DRAWS CLOSER AND CLOSER.
JUPITER WILL NEVER BE THE SAME
NOR WILL THE TWO SWEET SOULS.
                    AN INTERESTED PARTY

Once we were married,
King Geo sent out wedding
announcements and made an
official Jupiterian decree

THE KING DECREES:
THAT WHEREAS SHE IS
THE SWEETEST, MOST
BEAUTIFUL WOMAN
IN THE REALM; AND
WHEREAS SHE IS LOVED
BY HIM AS NO OTHER,
QUEEN SALLY BE
VENERATED FOREVER.

Hey Wonderful—

Wishing you lots of
    Tender Loving Care.

                    INSIDE MY SHORTS
Please Get ~~Well~~ Soon!

LOVE

        Your loving admirer,

        Mr. & Mrs. George Wade*

        * THE JUPITER TWINS

The wedding
announcement
of Mr. and Mrs.
George Wade—(i.e.
the Jupiter Twins)

And after that, Georgius-Jupiter Rex makes a private decree to his bride . . . replete with naked drawing.

WOW!!

THE KING LOVES HIS
QUEEN —
AND DECREES THAT SHE
SHALL RECEIVE ALL HIS
KISSES, TOUCHES, HUGS
AND LOVE FOREVERMORE
IN RETURN, HE WANTS
HER TO HOLD HIM IN HER
HEART FOR EVERY MOMENT
THEY'RE APART
GEORGIUS-JUPITER REX

— MR. CARLIN WADE
— MR. WADE WONDERFUL

MR. CARLIN WADE AND MR. WADE WONDERFUL

As you can see, on Jupiter, the man takes the woman's last name, instead of the woman taking his . . . *because I spoke up!* Geo's name was officially changed to Mr. Wade on the Jupiterian Registrar. In fact, after the wedding, Geo calls himself "Mr. Wade" here on Earth too. Unless we're trying to get better service in a restaurant or airport, of course—or we leave the house—and then it's "George Carlin as usual."

Here on Earth, Geo calls me his *"spouse without papers."* I'm his **Shackin' Up Overnight Honey.** Or he calls himself **"Sally's guy,"** and has it etched on the ankle bracelet I give him one year for Christmas.

I tried to get him to change his name to "Sally Wade." I said, "I'll take your name, but I need both the 'George' and the 'Carlin.' Not just 'Mrs. Carlin.' That way I'll get better service. You can have 'Sally Wade.' Although you won't get far with that name," I warned him. "I should know."

Geo tells Sal once: "If you ever want to use my name to get a table at a restaurant when I'm not around, feel free." I thought he meant it literally, so I changed my name to George Carlin long enough to make a couple of phone calls. (And I must say, it worked quite well.)

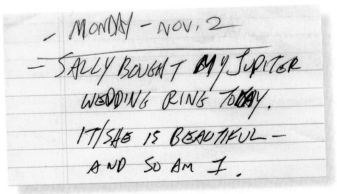

SALLY REGINA

NEXT TO YOU, THE SUN IS LIKE A MATCH, TEN THOUSAND MILES AWAY. YOU MAKE MY LIFE THAT BRIGHT. KEEP GROWING AND KEEP BEING YOU. LOVE, GEORGE

I called a doctor and the person with the answering service said, "The doctor's on sabbatical. We *never* give out his private number." So I lowered my voice and said,

"MY NAME IS GEORGE CARLIN—GIMME THE MOTHERFUCKIN' NUMBER." And they said, "707-555-7788."

Then I called a restaurant. "Well, we're completely booked," the hostess said. "We don't have anything before six a.m.; want to come in at six a.m. for breakfast?"

"This is George Carlin calling," I said. "*Mr. Wade Wonderful to you.*"

"Oh! Well, uhm—there is this one table suddenly available . . . right by the window! Most people fight over it, but we'll save it for you!"

AS THE KING ACCEPTED HIS RING FROM TIFFANY, HE WROTE:

- MONDAY - NOV. 2
- SALLY BOUGHT MY JUPITER WEDDING RING TODAY.
IT/SHE IS BEAUTIFUL -
AND SO AM I.

That's all that's necessary on Jupiter these days . . . although that may change in the future, who knows? There are no guarantees in outer space.

MY GIRL—
EXCLUSIVE PHOTOS SURFACE OF
SALLY AND GEO'S WEDDING KISS, AS
THE TWO NAKED LOVERS TIE THE KNOT
AND LOCK THEIR LIPS IN BELIZE OR
VENICE OR SPAIN OR SOMEWHERE IN
THE CARIBBEAN. THE WORLD CATCHES
FIRE WITH THE EXCITEMENT OF THE
HUGE JOY EXPLOSION CAUSED BY THEIR
LOVE STORM OF BRIGHT LIGHT-FILLED
BALLOONS RAINING DOWN SWEET, DEWY
JUICES OF SHEER, WONDERFUL SHINING
SPIRITS OF ~~*****~~ HARMONY AND HAPPI-
NESS. GEO. IS SO IN LOVE HE SINGS ALL
DAY LONG—SALLY'S JOY IS EXPRESSED IN
NON-STOP DANCING. THEY BOTH LOVE EACH
OTHER'S SINGIN' & DANCIN'—AND THEY LOVE
TO MAKE LOVE ON THE BEACH LATE
AT NIGHT, HALF IN THE WATER, UNDER
THE MOON, IN THE ARMS OF
JUPITER.

THE MAN

THE HONEYMOON

We honeymooned on Jupiter Island off the
coast of Key West, Florida. Jupiter Island is
what we call this partially submerged boat
with a tree growing out of it.

Back when the ocean was clean

I caught two fish after the ceremony. Geo's trying to make it look like he's the one that did, but I'm the one who actually caught the fish.

GEO KEEPS A RECORD OF THE HONEYMOON'S MORE MEMORABLE MOMENTS . . .

1,— GEO. PEEKED TWICE AT SALLY PEEING ON ISLAND.

HE LOVES YOU
HE LOVES YOU ~~NOT~~
HE LOVES YOU
HE LOVES YOU ~~NOT~~
HE LOVES YOU
HE LOVES YOU ~~NOT~~
HE LOVES YOU ....
OH, HI!
I LOVES YOU —
            GEO'GIE

Oh look, he finally caught one (with Captain Danny Sine)!

Sally —

I wish I could tell you —

I just don't know the words.

            George

my heart

        falls apart

kisses

        Baby

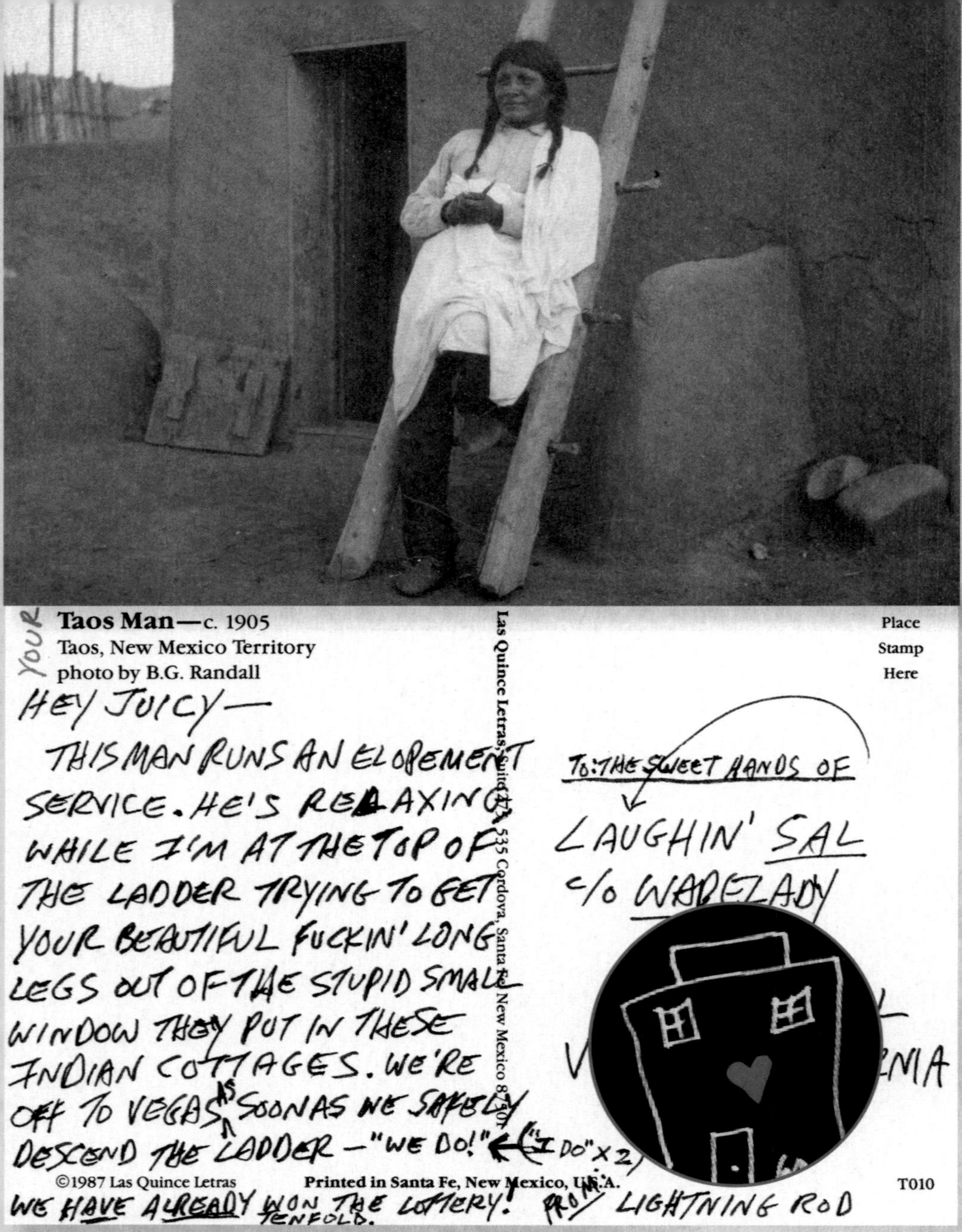
Taos Man—c. 1905
Taos, New Mexico Territory
photo by B.G. Randall
Place
Stamp
Here
Las Quince Letras, Suite 7A, 535 Cordova, Santa Fe, New Mexico 87501
©1987 Las Quince Letras
Printed in Santa Fe, New Mexico, U.S.A.
T010
YOUR
HEY JUICY—
THIS MAN RUNS AN ELOPEMENT SERVICE. HE'S RELAXING WHILE I'M AT THE TOP OF THE LADDER TRYING TO GET YOUR BEAUTIFUL FUCKIN' LONG LEGS OUT OF THE STUPID SMALL WINDOW THEY PUT IN THESE INDIAN COTTAGES. WE'RE OFF TO VEGAS AS SOON AS WE SAFELY DESCEND THE LADDER — "WE DO!" "I DO" x 2
WE HAVE ALREADY WON THE LOTTERY! TENFOLD.
FROM LIGHTNING ROD
TO: THE SWEET HANDS OF
LAUGHIN' SAL
c/o WADELADY

CHAPTER 10½

Jupiter Geo & Sal: The Wedding Album

Geo makes this wedding album for Sal as a keepsake.

Mule Team — c. 1900
Chihuahua, Mexico
photo by B.G. Randall

HEY GOOFS!

THE WEDDING LIMOUSINE CARRYING LENORE & MARTHA & JIM TAKES A WRONG TURN AT BRANSON AND THE 3 OF THEM DECIDE TO STAY AND WATCH THE TONY ORLANDO SHOW, THEREBY MISSING THE WEDDING. THEY WANDER IN THE DESERT FOR SEVERAL YEARS, FINALLY SETTLING DOWN AND RAISING FROZEN CORN AND PEAS. JIM MARRIES A SQUAW, MARTHA COMMITS SUICIDE, AND LENORE WRITES A BOOK ENTITLED, "NOW, SALLY..." — GEESK!

SALLY PAL

Taos Girls — c. 1905
Taos, New Mexico Territory
photo by B.G. Randall

TO YOU — FROM ME (WITH GREAT LOVE)

TWO OF THE BRIDESMAIDS FROM THE BIG WEDDING TURNED UP TODAY IN DEEPEST ARIZONA. THEY HAD BEEN GIVEN THE WRONG ADDRESS FOR THE RECEPTION AND HAD WANDERED OVER 600 MILES BEFORE BECOMING DISORIENTED AND HAVING "SACRED VISIONS" OF A LARGE GASEOUS PLANET WITH A BIG RED SPOT. THE KING AND QUEEN APPEARED TO THEM AND GAVE THEM VITAMINS AND OATMEAL COOKIES AND SQUIRTED A FOUL, BROWN FLUID INTO THEIR

SEXYWADE

T011

Printed in Santa Fe, New Mexico, U.S.A.

SWEET

—GOLDEN LIGHT:
SALLY GETS ANGRY AT GEORGE
WHEN SHE DISCOVERS THAT
THE USHERS HE HIRED FOR THE
WEDDING ARE ACTUALLY 8 NAKED
WOMEN HOLDING BIG FLOWERS ON
THEIR FACES. GEORGE EXPLAINS
THAT THE WASN'T RESPONSIBLE
BECAUSE HE TOOK A SLEEPING
PILL. SALLY LAUGHS AND FORGOES
A DIET COKE FOR A FRUIT DRINK.
THEY KISS AND SOMETIMES SLEEP
FOR A LONG TIME. THEN THEY
LAUGH SOME MORE. ——>YOUR MAN —> GCOCKLIN

WADE LADY!

11 West 53 Street, New York, NY 10019

USA 01   19 USA
American Kestrel

A TRAIN CARRYING CHAM-
PAGNE IN TANKER CARS
NEVER REACHES THE WED-
DING PARTY, BECAUSE A
DEAF COCKER SPANIEL
CROSSES THE TRACK AND
SPOOKS THE ENGINEER.
THE DOG WAS NOT INJURED
BUT HE GOT DRUNK LAPPING
UP CHAMPAGNE AND STARTED
DANCING
AROUND
LIKE
LINDA BLAIR, THROWING HIMSELF AGAINST DOORS.

SWEET WADE

"Thousands of Dollars Go Up in Smoke in Kansas."
1928. "The blazing wreck of a train of twenty-seven
cars filled with gasoline, which burned after a smash
near Zyba." Times Wide World Photos. © The New
York Times

CHAPTER 11

The Lewd Chapter

HEY SHOWER GIRL—
YOU'RE MY
QUEEN,
AND I WORSHIP
YOU. ALSO YOU'RE
A REAL COOL
LADY.
YOUR FARTING GUY
GEO!

HEY,
COOKIE!
I WENT OUT
TO FIND MONEY
+ BUY TAMPONS.
LOVE,
YOUR GUY

People say George is
fearless.

That's true. Even in love that's true.

I find this out one day when we enter a drugstore and I let him go up to the counter for me, so I don't embarrass myself, after whispering to him that I needed some feminine hygiene products. So he walks up to the counter, and in a loud voice says, "Where's the tampon section? How much is that vaginal cream? Is that on special? Where's that stuff for anal warts? Gimme three—one for myself and two for my asshole buddies! Where's that suppository section? You want the super plus? Hon? I don't see the lubricants!"

Then, perusing the shelf . . . "And while you're at it, throw in some Vagisil Medicated Anti-Itch Wipes as a present to my gal, Sal. That oughta feel good on that sweet butt o' yours."

HE'S INFORMATIVE AS WELL AS ROMANTIC.

In the middle of the night, he says, "I need to blow a big fart and then I'll be right back." Not many guys'll tell you that. It's rare. Then when he gets back, he says, "Did ya miss me?"

Then he says, "Oops, gotta light a match now. That way you won't know I farted."

That's really romantic. That's how you know you're really loved.

When I open a window, he says, "I thought you wouldn't notice. It'll pass in a week or two. I didn't know it was gonna be like that! C'mon! Lighten up! I thought it would be neutral and pass unnoticed! Nothing preceded it! In fact, maybe it'll spread the stench to let the dog upstairs too!"

Then he leaves again, returns, and frowns. "What's the matter?" I ask.

"Every time I go into the bathroom to fart—it isn't there."

I tell him to write that one down, it's so romantic . . . (one more for the Jupiter box.)

Then he announces, "I gotta go pee now." He leaves, comes back, and says, "I'm done peeing now! . . . Did you miss me? . . . My pee's over now."

I'm thinkin', *In the length of time it takes to pee, how much can you miss somebody?*

JUPITER

Ev time I go in the B.R. to fart — it isn't there

Hi COOKIE —
I GOT THE BEDROOM READY FOR YA.
AND YA LOOK BEE-YOU-TEE-FUL!
MR CAKE

MY PANTS CAN COME OFF REAL EASILY —

More **foreplay** by Geo

- One day, when I told Geo I was gonna take a hot bath before sex, he said, "Ya wouldn't wash a sandwich, would ya?"

- Nothing like working with a little woody to keep you company.

- You can give it a little yank if you're not too tired.

- Watch out or you're gonna fall outta bed and we don't need that!

GEO:
The candle looks great with the flowers.

SAL:
Yeah, I know.

GEO: *Your* **leg waxing** *was a very successful event.* I LIKED IT VERY MUCH.

SAL: THANK YOU.

Maybe in some other universe, this would be a turn-on . . .

I would live with you a thousand years — just to smell your asshole.

Hey, Goofy? What Goofy? WhErE the fuck arE all the pussy eating Candles?

- I thought about leaving this out . . . but it is a book about George Carlin . . . so I just shrank it down . . .

YER GONNA GET A BAGEL

HEY—

BONUS NOTE—

I HOPE TO SUCK YOUR TOES REAL SOON.

—ME

TO TYPING LADY,

SOMEDAY, WHEN WE'RE WORKING LIKE THIS IN YOUR BEDROOM, REMIND ME TO COME OVER AND FUCK YOU.

The Guy In The ~~Box~~ Next Cubicle.

Bonus note!

YOU SURE LOOK FINE. NICE HINEY!

Poetry works well with most women, if ya wanna copy this one down . . .

JUST GRAB IT ONCE— for A FEW SECONDS.

PLEASE

IT'S A DATE, MATE! I THINK IT'S GRATE. WE'LL FORNI-CATE. WE'LL "SALI" VATE. ~~AND WE'LL MAS~~ AND WE'LL MASTI-CATE TILL IT GETS REAL LATE JUST DON'T MENSTRU-ATE.

Ex-o-lent! Why, thank ya, ma'am!

A PRIVATE PARTS SEGMENT

One evening, Geo finds a piece of carrot on his private parts. He says, "What's this doin' there? Didya have it in your hand?"

I said, "I don't know—maybe the dog coughed it up."

"Don't worry," he said. "It's chock full of vitamin A, which I've heard is a natural aphrodisiac."

I said, "Yeah . . . vitamin A. In fact, it works better than . . . what's that sex drug called?"

"Yeah, I know the one you mean," he says. "Not Valium, but that other one."

"Viagra," I say. "Valium and Viagra. I always get those two mixed up."

"Well, that's because they both start with 'V,'" Geo explains. "That's why."

Hey, it may not be funny, but Geo's proud of me. I can hear him say now, "Ya can't go wrong with a private parts segment, Sarree Jane! Yaaay, S.J.! Ya included a private parts segment! Just for Geo'gie!"

This card seems pretty straightforward, until you get to the ending . . .

My own sweet bright light, Sally:

These trees are still young and new but already strong and sturdy — and with a long life-span ahead of them. JUST LIKE OUR LOVE

They are also bathed in a golden glow — as I am, when I'm in your presence. Your love bathes me in warm, golden wonderfulness.

Your baby, PUMPKIN BALLS

CHAPTER 12

Trouble in the Bubble

Trouble In the Bubble

Two lovers miss each other
very much;
they are deeply committed at many
many levels.
They are close — but pulled apart.
It hurts a lot. It really hurts.
Add to that the LIMITATIONS
of the TELEPHONE, and you have
the perfect ~~formula~~ BREEDING GROUND for trouble
in the bubble; for lovers to
be hurt some more.
              I'm sorry —
                    I love you,
                         George

SAC & GEO
"GET YER FUCKIN
HORMONES IN ORDER,
WILL YA? IT'S LIKE
LIVIN' WITH A
CHEMISTRY
   SET."

CHEER
THE
FUCK
UP!

GRUMPS

HOLDIN' ON WITH ONE HAND.

...SED OFF TO YOU —

I DON'T ALWAYS
HANDLE THINGS RIGHT.
I'M SORRY.
I'M LEARNING.
ALL IN ALL, I'M
A PRETTY
COOL GUY TO
BE WITH.

BEAR WITH ME.
I GET NOTHING
BUT BETTER.

FROM ME

Someone once said to me,
**"I don't know how anyone
can win an argument
with GEORGE CARLIN."**
That's true.

Sally —
I hope you know you
are my whole love, my only
love and my forever love —
that's just the way it is, and
it will always be. I'm sorry
if I ever hurt you; I never
meant to do that. But I would
rather I hurt you by saying too
much than by saying too little.
Please forgive me. George

In fact, Geo is so skillful
with words, he can
genuinely apologize in
such a way as to still be
in the right.

SARA—

I KNOW YOU'RE TRYIN' TO HANDLE A LOT OF BIG THINGS — ALL THE WHILE HAVING A LOT OF PAIN AND DISCOMFORT. JUST LET ME KNOW HOW I CAN HELP IN THE BEST WAYS FOR YOU, AND I'LL DO IT. I'LL WAIT TO TAKE YOUR CUES. JUST KNOW MOST OF MY "CHATTER" IS TOWARD GOOD ENDS, MY STYLE SUCKS + IT'S HARD TO CHANGE SOME

THING AS BASIC AS STYLE. THE IMPROVEMENTS I'VE MADE ALONG THOSE LINES LARGELY GO UNNOTICED → BECAUSE THEY ARE AN ABSENCE, NOT A PRESENCE, THEREFORE NOT VISIBLE.

BUT BELIEVE ME, THEY'RE THERE.

I'LL BE DOWNSTAIRS — LUVIN' YOU MORE THAN EVER.

We loved each other so much, even when we were together, we missed each other. We missed each other if we were in the same room, working on separate projects, knowing our minds had gone in different directions. We'd gaze at each other, and sigh. **We'd talk, all night sometimes,** instead of sleeping. Especially if the light from the moon shined through the window, or Jupiter was nearby.

But other times, we'd argue over whose line was funnier, like dueling banjos. And when we'd get angry, we'd refrain from laughing at one another's jokes—just like the Democrats and Republicans who refuse to vote "yes" on the other party's issues. In fact, being stone-faced and sullen was the biggest punishment either of us could think of to bestow on one another.

SOMETIMES GEORGE STEPS ON MY LINES.

AND SOMETIMES I STEP ON HIS LINES. HE LETS ME KNOW WHEN I DO THAT.

Geo lets Sal know she's stepping on his lines.

HIS BOUNDARIES WEREN'T ALWAYS CLEAR . . .

Once, Geo deleted the outgoing message on my answering machine when he was trying to fix the machine while I was gone—and he erased the best outgoing message I ever had. I told him I wouldn't have fixed his machine without asking. I was angry because I couldn't remember exactly what I'd said on the recording that was so great, nor could I get the right inflection in my voice again. Probably because I was **PISSED OFF.**

"Better than **pissed on,**" he says.

I bitched to my guru, Jack, who explained, "There are two take-charge people in your house. What did you expect?" Then Geo would feel bad because he'd feel I didn't appreciate his good intentions. Shit like that.

aughlin, 1984

HEY GOOFY!
THIS IS WHAT
YOU LOOK LIKE
WHEN YOU GET MAD
MR. PERFECT

Distributed by TANGIBLES PO Box 547 Ranchos de Taos, NM 8

THE PERFECT ARGUMENT [4]

Afterward, he'd apologize. He was very apologetic. He'd just say he was sorry, that he'd never do it again. He'd never mess with it—whatever *it* was—without asking me again. Or, until the next time it needed fixing. Then I'd feel bad that I hurt his feelings, and neither of us would learn anything except that *we loved each other more than we did before.* That's the only lesson there is anyway in life. If there's another one, we missed it.

The following is a **Jupiter story** the twins write,

to pull themselves out of an argument. I pretend I'm him (Cake) talking to me (Cookie), and he pretends that he's me talking to him.

SAL: *Dear Cookie,*
I apologize for bein' so mean to you since you drove all this way to see me. Ain't you cute!
Love, Cake

GEO: *Dear Cake,*
Thank you for your wonderful note, but you are on the wrong track.

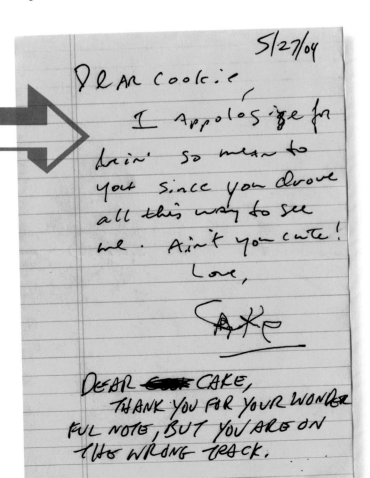

5/27/04

Dear Cookie,

I appolosize for bein' so mean to you since you drove all this way to see me. Ain't you cute!

Love,

Cake

Dear ~~Cook~~ Cake,
Thank you for your wonderful note, but you are on the wrong track.

IT IS I WHO SHOULD BE MAKING AMENDS TO YOU — YOU MAGNIFICENT MAN. I WAS RESPONSIBLE FOR THE FRICTION AT DINNER —I WAS SIMPLY FRUSTRATED AT NOT BEING ABLE TO UNDRESS YOU RIGHT THEN AND THERE AND HAVE MY WAY WITH YOU. I THINK TONIGHT IS HEADING IN A BETTER DIRECTION EVEN THO' I'M TIRED. WELL, THERE'S ALWAYS TOMORROW MORNING. LOVE COOKIE

GEO AS SAL: *It is I who should be making amends to YOU—you magnificent man. I was responsible for the friction at dinner—I was simply frustrated at not being able to undress you right then and there and have my way with you. I think tonight is heading in a better direction, even tho' I'm tired. Well, there's always tomorrow morning. Love,*

Cookie

You're MY EVERYTHING

THIS IS WHAT SARA JANE LOOKED LIKE THE OTHER NIGHT.

....AND I LOVE HER VERY MUCH.

from
— MEAN LITTLE GEORGIE

IN FACT, MOST OF OUR ARGUMENTS ARE ON PAPER . . .

I read his "men/women" routine on a plane, and he's hurt by my response. He likes it when we agree on what he writes. Also, he wants me to know that I'm his equal—if not his superior—intellectually, creatively, and in every other way. But once during an airplane flight, we argue on paper about "a civilization that's male-bred and sustained by male violence," as he takes the woman's point of view.

I was in a snit. A HISSY FIT, I guess you'd call it.

I'm sorry now that I was upset when I read what he wrote, and that I told him to have a "good show and a nice life" without me. It was a ridiculous argument, but as you can see, we recovered nicely, and he voices his viewpoint on a male-dominated society.

I'M ONLY TRYING TO BE A SMALL VOICE OF DISSENT AMONG THE MAN-WORSHIPPER AMONG US. I SWING A HEAVY BLADE THAT DOESN'T ALLOW FOR EXCEPTIONS AND DISCLAIMERS. THAT'S THE WAY I EVEN

SOME MEN ARE "SENSITIVE" AND SOME WOMEN ARE "REAL CUNTS." THE POINT IS, THIS HEAP OF SHIT WE CALL CIVILIZATION IS MALE-BRED AND SUSTAINED BY MALE VIOLENCE. I WILL NEVER

THE SCORE FOR ALL THE HORRIBLE SHIT VISITED ON ALL OF US BY THE DOMINANT, WESTERN, MECHANIZED CULTURE OF MALE SUPERIORITY AND CRUELTY. I DON'T GIVE A FUCK THAT

APOLOGIZE FOR MY PERCEPTIONS AND PASSIONATE THOUGHT.* AND YES, I WILL HAVE A GOOD SHOW AND A NICE LIFE.

* I WILL, HOWEVER, APOLOGIZE FOR MISJUDGING YOUR FEELINGS ON THIS SUBJECT.

In retrospect, I shouldn't have written him this . . .

I'm going to live by myself the rest of my life . . I want nothin' else to do with man . . the world.

moi →

But as **Jupiterians,**
we both like forgiving
ourselves.

Especially for something we don't find fault with in the first place. We do that real quick, in fact, as soon as possible.

REGARDLESS of all the stupid shit that crops up, we're still the cutest people on the plane — and the sweetest.

On the flight home, I write him a final note about the argument, which reads:

Dear Geo,
Allow me to express my feelings without dumping them on you. I'm tired, I ate too much, my hormones are screwy, and I broke my New Year's resolution about drinking Diet Coke. I think it would be better if you slept at your place.
Love,
Sal

HEY FACE-MAKER —

IT'S REALLY ALL O.K. IT JUST DOESN'T FEEL LIKE IT ALL THE TIME.

PLEASE GIVE YOURSELF A BREAK FOR THE 11 HOURS WE HAVE LEFT IN NY.

151 WEST 54TH STREET, NEW YORK, NEW YORK 10019
(212) 307-5000

— A FELLOW FACE-MAKER

So Geo slept at his place—it was my place too.

For a real argument, it would take us separating—one of us going for a drive, one of us doing something for twenty minutes, or an hour. Once, we pretended like we were splitting up. He gets up from the computer, grabs his purse—*he likes calling his bag a purse 'cause most men don't*—then grabs a suitcase and leaves. But he doesn't put anything in the suitcase . . . and it isn't his suitcase, it's mine. That's how I know he's not going far.

Planning ahead, before he goes, Geo makes himself two turkey sandwiches with his special low-sodium fake salt to take with him, as if he's running away from home. Then he gets in his car, drives around the block a few times, calls me on his cell, text messages me, sends me two or three emails, comes back home, gives me a kiss, then **eats one of his turkey sandwiches and gives the other one to Spot.** To this day, Spot says that's the only time he's ever been tricked. He thought he'd lost the best personal assistant he'd ever had, and he blamed the whole damn thing on me.

Geo, driving around with an empty suitcase, calling Sal on the phone . . . finding out what's for dinner

Dear Oats,

IF YOU LIVE BY YOURSELF, SPOT WILL MISS ME. AND I WILL MISS YOU. AND I'LL HAVE TO GO HANG OUT WITH A BUNCH OF TESTOSTERONE GUYS.

PLEASE RECONSIDER. BARLEY MAN

SA

HANG IN THERE,
BABY,
HORMONES COME
AND GO, BUT TRUE
LOVE LASTS
FOREVER.

- AND YOU'RE
DOIN' FINE.

Sally my dear, my love —
This doggie has come to personally load up any bad feelings you have left and drive them to the Hudson River + dump them in. Please never let a stray sentence or two put you in a bad spot. My devotion to you is COMPLETE!! GOT THAT? COMPLETE. LIKE You.

YOUR
SERVANT
IN
LOVE

A card Geo reminds me to read whenever he unintentionally hurts my feelings

HI BEE-BEE!
DOCTOR EINSTEIN ATTEMPTS TO
QUANTIFY THE LOVE THAT FLOWS
BACK AND FORTH BETWEEN THE
TWO GREAT JUPITERIAN LOVERS,
SAL + GEO. I'VE GOT A CLUE FOR
HIM — HIS FINGERS WILL NOT DO!
NOR WILL THOSE EQUATIONS ON
THE BLACKBOARD BEHIND HIM.
WHAT HE MUST DO IS TO START TO
COUNT ELECTRONS, PROTONS,
NEUTRONS AND THE MANY SUB-ATOMIC
PARTICLES SUCH AS MUONS, GLUONS,
QUARKS, MESONS, BOSONS, — ALL
THE SUB-ATOMIC PARTICLES HE CAN
CONCEIVE OF THAT EVER EXISTED
IN ALL TIME — AND MULTIPLY THAT
BY THE NUMBER OF RAISINS IN CAL-
IFORNIA — THEN YOU HAVE A START.

QUINT BUCHHOLZ · ALBERT EINSTEIN   2008   EDITION Inkognito · ERKELENZDAMM 11-13 · 10 44

LOVE FOREVER — JULES

TO:
C/O WADE
LADY SILK
MY SWEETIE
4/
V

CHAPTER 13

Relationship Axioms
from Jupiter

THE JUPITER TWINS CREATE A SERIES OF RULES TO LIVE BY CALLED "AXIOMS."

Sometimes they are like meditations—they transcend romantic relationships, and are more like life advice. We call it "bubble work," because we see ourselves traveling through time in a bubble together. Even though we each have our own point of view, we are both more committed to the bubble than we are to ourselves individually.

A FEW EXAMPLES OF JUPITERIAN AXIOMS

THE EVER-EXPANDING, INFINITE BUBBLE OF LOVE

HOW IMPORTANT IS THIS TO YOU?

THE VALLEYS ARE WHEN WE'RE OUT of PRESENT TIME + NEED TO LOCATE OURSELVES + ASK FOR EACH OTHER'S HELP.

LOOK WHO'S DANCING IN A BUBBLE.

Wording by Sal & Geo, although written down by Geo with artwork by him

AXIOM STAY IN Courtship mode

HOW IMPORTANT IS THIS TO US? * RE: AN ARGUMENT FORMING

THIS IS A WONDER IN PROGRESS.

153

When I first come home, Sally might tend to be a little "standoffish" because of old patterns she had in her FORMER LONG-DISTANCE relationships. GO AHEAD and KID her a little about it — COACH HER to realize it's an old pattern.

SUPPER

(THURS.)

REASSURE AND COMPLIMENT SALLY ALL DAY LONG.
I GOT DEGRUMPED BY SALLY

ALWAYS DEGRUMPIFY THE OTHER PERSON

TRY NOT TO START AN ARGUMENT DURING A CIRCUS. (NIGHTTIME)

Jupiter Island in the far right-hand distance again

Sal keeps track of this habit and feels there's too steep a learning curve to change it.

RESPONSES WHEN REPEATING

"where'd I hear that last?" ~~is that~~ ~~something I said.~~ ~~did~~

"COULD I HAVE SAID THAT?"

"I LOVE what you say too!"

"That sounds like something I MIGHT'VE SAID."

TIMES I don't listen, continue my thought -- then say what you just suggested

SUN	MON	TUES	WED.	THURS	FRI	SAT
				✓	✓	✓
✓	✓	✓	✓	✓	✓	✓
✓	✓	✓	✓	✓		
✓	✓	✓	✓			

AXIOM EXERCISE:
HAVE EACH ARGUMENT LEAD TO AN AXIOM

AXIOM → BY THIS TIME, NO ARGUMENT SHOULD EVER INCLUDE ANY KIND OF REFERENCE # TO ENDING THE RELATIONSHIP. I'M NOT REALISTIC.

GEORGE HAS TO LEARN TO DISTANCE HIMSELF from CONTROLLING and TO CONTROL HIS DISTANCING.

Stop

I'M OKAY
to hear
anything you
have to
SAY NOW.

GO

RR AXIOM #2
RIHGA ROYAL HOTEL
NEW YORK

It's out of character
for us to argue with
each other — we've
got our feel with the
rest of the ~~world~~ WORLD...
....It's out of character!!!

Geo,
FROM TIME TO TIME,
PULL SALLY OUT
OF "THE PROCESS"
AND
ME TOO.

FROM OUR AXIOM FOLDER . . .

Sometimes the axioms are only for me, sometimes they are only for Geo, sometimes they are for the two of us. We would both come up with them, but we'd often word them together and agree on the final version. We felt we were teaching them back on Jupiter how to live—essentially by showing them how to get along on this planet, under the worst possible conditions.

X For one week a month, don't assess anything. Let it float. And don't throw in the towel.

X On stress days, don't put into the Mixmaster any innocent comment by Geo.

X While traveling, no serious topics discussed. Especially over the phone. Because you say to yourself, *Now there's silence. Well, does that mean he's pouting or does that mean he's agreeing with me . . .*

X Help Geo while still incipient.

X Be Sal instead of doing something.

X Stay in present time.

X Neither Geo nor Sal is perfect.

X Assess Geo on his own level.

x Any flowers will do.

X **FROM SAL TO GEO** (*worded with his input*): I understand you're tired and stressed, but don't act like a temperamental child.

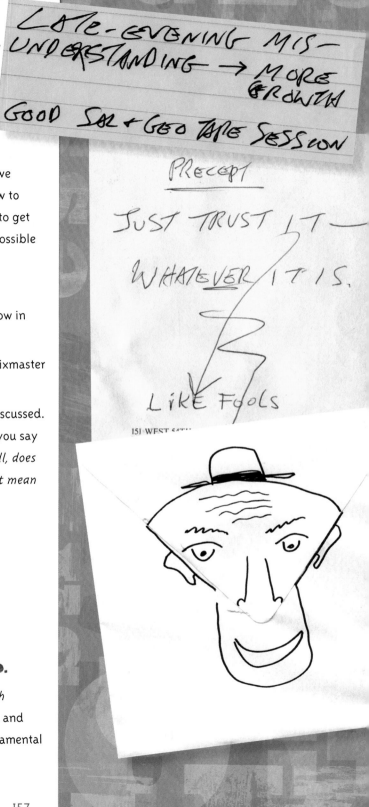

157

"JUPITER TO SALLY..."

If she forgets WHAT I SAID, SAY, "WHAT are you THINKING RIGHT NOW?"

WHEN NOT UNDERSTANDING OTHER PERSON'S INTENT & MEANING:

AXIOM "Let me check with you on this:"

✘ Overreacting. It's happening! Let's drop it!

✘ Cheer up! Yer in love!

✘ Assume innocence!

✘ **Geo to Sal:** If Sally's feelings are hurt, ask George his intentions instead of reacting too hastily.

✘ **Geo to Sal:** Say, "Yes, sir—General, sir!" if Geo is bossy.

✘ Even in argument, ask self: "Does this nurture the relationship and come from the heart?"

✘ Give Geo benefit of doubt.

✘ Let's talk about this later because it's something that requires thought and I need to stay focused.

✘ *Prefaces are important!* Example: I don't know if this is the right time to bring this up, and you might think it needs more time for discussion than I do. So I'll say it anyway and you can tell me and we both get a vote.

✘ Light touch.

✘ Choose your battles!

✘ Take a walk!

Note 1 (top left, handwritten)

Q's for GEO DURING "IT" *

- WHO'S IN CHARGE HERE?

- WHO SHOULD BE IN CHARGE HERE?

- WHAT DO YOU NEED FROM ME RIGHT THIS MINUTE?

GEO: * FIXIN' THINGS vs. SAL'S FEELINGS

↓ to 'listen, maybe humor me Or to ask an interested question or two.

DON'T INTERPRET QUIET SUPPORT AS OPPOSITION OR ANTAGONISM. LET ME HEAR YOU QUIETLY WITH A SUPPORTIVE COMMENT OR TWO.

Note 2 (top right, handwritten)

SAL

AXIOM X—
"what's eatin' you?"

Note 3 (right, handwritten)

PRESENT TIME!!

DON'T PROJECT BAD THINGS — CAREER OR PERSONAL — LIVE IN THE JOY AND HAPPINESS OF NOW. WHATEVER MIGHT BE OUT THERE ISN'T REAL.

Printed list

✖ Lesson for Geo concerning a joke of Sal's:
Hang on—hang on—I'd like that to come first on my own. Can you let that come from me? To rise out of her autonomous independence.

✖ Lesson for Geo taking charge of Sal's material:
Back off, but still be **supportive.**

✖ Be on guard as to where you're coming from.

✖ Don't make *their* problem *your* problem.

✖ Be willing to admit to anything—"I was dumb, stupid—I apologize."

SIGNS WE HOLD UP . . . AS YOU CAN SEE, THEY BOTH AMOUNT TO THE SAME THING.

SAL (who thinks Geo is sounding like her father), dismissed!

GEO (who thinks Sal is sounding like his mother), chastised!

GOOFY#2

Dismissed

(chastised)

GOOFY#1

ORDERED

(chastised)

A ROUGH SORT OF UNSENTIMENTAL HONESTY

Hey, Sallus!

Axiom #2

This is Monday, 2:35 AM — ten or fifteen minutes after you called back to say, "It's out of character for us to argue with each other — our beef is with the rest of the world ... it's out of character!" (Routine) You're, such a sweet genius.

Sally, I have to tell you — one of the things (only one — there are so many) about you that continues to astonish and challenge me is your COMPLETE commitment to a ROUGH sort of UNSENTIMENTAL HONESTY. THAT IS A COMPLIMENT. I IGNORE THE NEGATIVE TONE OF THE WORDS "ROUGH" and "UNSENTIMENTAL." YOU CHALLENGE ME, AND I FIND MYSELF QUESTION- ING MY OWN CREDENTIALS. I PRIDE MYSELF ON A

Just as Geo sees through every institution, we've **never considered ourselves to be part of any group.** We aren't joiners, contributors, or affiliated with any organizations—we are all about each other's love. And because we have an amazing ability to connect intellectually, creatively, and spiritually, together we were on a journey to learn how to best communicate emotionally.

CERTAIN LEVEL OF PERSONAL HONESTY — AND I

DON'T THINK IT'S MISPLACED, BUT ON CONFRONTING

YOU DURING ~~THE~~ OUR 'ARGUMENT' LAST SUNDAY

I REALIZED I WAS BEING SOMEWHAT DISHONEST.

THE WHOLE TONE OF WHAT I WAS DOING SEEMED

FALSE TO ME. CAN'T PUT MY FINGER ON IT — AND I

DON'T CARE IF I FIGURE IT OUT OR NOT. JUST ^NOTICING IT

AT ALL IS MORE IMPORTANT, I THINK.

    ANYWAY, ~~THIS~~ I HAVE AN IDEA FOR AN

AXIOM #3 THAT I WANT TO TALK TO YOU

ABOUT. MAYBE IT WOULD HELP AS MUCH AS

#1 already HAS and as ~~much as~~ MUCH AS #2

seems to promise.

        I'LL CUT THIS SHORT NOW.

(I HAVE SO MUCH MORE TO SAY TO YOU IN THIS LETTER

FORM, THAT IT'S FRUSTRATING TO JUST DO A SHORT NOTE.)

I WOULD LOVE TO ESTABLISH A LOVE-LETTER CORRES-

PONDENCE WITH YOU, SALLY

                THE MAN WITH
                THE PEN —
                G. CARLIN

MS + SAL

WE'RE IN

PRESENT

TIME.

More axioms

Geo.
I think we
should go to A
nice restaurant,
with A jupiter
story & have a
date nite once a
week. Don't
you? yes [X] x x x
check here No [ ]

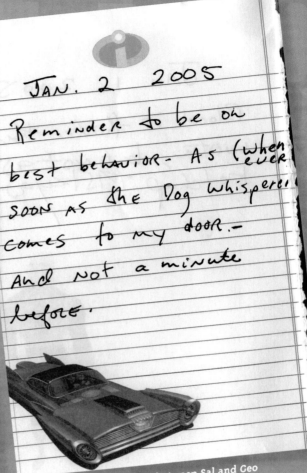

JAN. 2 2005
Reminder to be on
best behavior. As (when-
ever) soon as the Dog whisperer
comes to my door. —
And not a minute
before.

Spot's axiom, as mediator between Sal and Geo

Axiom # 10
The person
who is the
least angry
puts the cork
back in the
wine bottle.

| AXIOM |

After a separation — set aside immed-iate time to spend together. That day and/or the next day or two. RE-ESTABLISH the INTIMACY.

BOTTOM LINE
AXIOM

There are any number of things that can run away with (OUR) your thoughts and make (US) you a little crazy — the future, our careers, where we live, How we live — but the "BOTTOM LINE" is — we're going to fall asleep in each other's arms.

Sally & Greg TOGETHER should both get the Nobel Peace Prize — based on how they work on their "problems."

Sally —
The important thing is that we love each other. All the rest is/

Hey Sweetie!

I'm on the plane. Almost
two hours, now. I can't see
Jupiter, but guess who's peekin'
in my window? SIRIUS!

I got 3 hours to go. I'm
gonna sleep soon. I've been
working on my show — fixing things,
finding sequences, all that stuff.
It feels good. I haven't worked
on my shit for awhile. I'm gonna
have to do a little more as these
weeks come on. As of December
first I only have 31 shows left
to do until HBO. Somehow, it
seems awful short, but I know
I can get done what I need. It's
gonna feel good to go with stuff
that's only recently developed. My
patterns are changing — guess
why? 'Cause I love you — that's
what. And it's good — good for me.
GOOD FOR US. LOVE GEORGE

CHAPTER 14

Food and Dining

The other day someone said to me, **"I loved listening to him rant, about the bullshit stuff that goes on in this world...he always hit the nail right on the head."**

I'm thinking to myself, *Yeah. True! But he was also a big baby who'd only eat canned peas instead of fresh, because they've got sugar on them.*

And not to say Geo's food preferences were a tad pedestrian, but he would drain the mushrooms out of a can of mushroom soup before he'd eat it. The first time I offered him popcorn, his knee-jerk response was, "Don't push me," because he wasn't sure if it had butter on it or not, and he doesn't like it without it.

Before he met me, his manager and best friend, Jerry Hamza, said that Geo only ate only butter noodles, as opposed to "spaghetti" or "pasta with sauce." "Drawn butter," Geo clarifies, then draws.

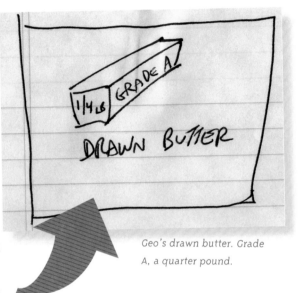

Geo's drawn butter. Grade A, a quarter pound.

Plus, he thinks turkey tastes like bad sneakers. **"Insoles,"** he says. And he doesn't like pickles, onions, or olives. "Ham and bacon in pea soup are okay though," he says, "once I got in the air force."

Even though we go to the same restaurant, we eat entirely different food. I order grilled fish and vegetables, he orders meatloaf, mashed potatoes, and cooked carrots. **"Comfort food,"** he says—which is another way of saying **"not good for you."** Then he'd dip the white bread in olive oil and talk about how good olive oil was for him, hoping I'd be proud of him. I was proud of him. But not for dipping white bread in olive oil.

Ewwwww . . . goose liver.

After a while, he begins to implicitly trust my food choices, and will try anything off my fork—even though I lie to him about *foie gras*. *I tell him foie gras is mushrooms instead of goose liver so he'll like it.*

The first time he tastes raw fish, I don't know what he thinks it is, but since he knows I wouldn't feed him raw fish, he eats it. I only tell him it's raw fish after he says he likes it; otherwise, I would have said it was chicken.

After a few years, he begins experimenting on his own. A bad idea, I caution. And at times I have to warn him: "Don't order that *squid,* you won't like it." Or, "*Octopus* has a chewy texture. You might want the filet mignon. It's so tender, you can cut it with a fork."

RIPPED FROM THE HEADLINES OF THE *JUPITER BLAT!*

A page of a Jupiter story, this one written by Geo at a sushi restaurant called the Hard Rock Café in Vegas . . .

RIGHT OFF THE BAT, GEO. FOUND HIMSELF IN "HOT-SAKE." *HIS "LITTLE GEO."* WAS ON THE LOOSE AND CAUSING TROUBLE AT DINNER. FIRST THE CHOPSTICKS, THEN THE SAKE, THEN THE SOUP, THEN THE SALAD DRESSING — JEEZ! HE KEPT SENDIN' OUT BAD SIGNALS & SAL WAS GETTIN' STEAMED. SHE WENT TO TAKE A PEE & TAKE A LOOK AT SOME OF THE GUITARS WHILE "LITTLE GEO" GREW UP AND ORDERED AN ACTUAL LIVING FISH WHICH HE WAS FORCED TO EAT AS IT ACTUALLY SWAM AROUND IN A TANK, USING ONLY HIS HANDS AND HIS TEETH. HE SILENTLY PRAYED FOR CHICKEN.

Georgie wants a nice bowl of pasta - NO EEL or shrimp or octopus. Light oil. 40 weight or under

Sometimes I order for Geo before he gets there,

and there's very little time because of an impending show, so I read this note with instructions to the waiter—that way I know he'll be pleased by the results he gets.

NO BLUE FOOD

You know how George has a routine called "No Blue Food"? Well, one night at dinner, I point out that blueberries are blue, but he claims they're purple. When we ask around the restaurant, everyone agrees with me. He shows his displeasure by clamming up and acting as if he's been mortally wounded. I feel terrible, as if I've ruined the pinnacle of his entire life's work—until I share my dessert with him, which is blueberry pie with whipped cream. Then suddenly he perks up, and it's okay with him that there is blue food. But for a while, I was worried.

There IS blue food . . . hmm.

If soup was filling and helped curb your appetite, then so would drinking water, he points out.

If either one of us was **ME + SAL** *in charge of the food — neither of us would ever eat, because the other one would get it all all the food.*

One Night in New York:

The Restaurant Story

While eating a lovely dinner in a nice restaurant—global cuisine, a little pinot. . . . I notice I'm with a guy who coughs stuff up, swallows it the wrong way—and then tells you about it.

Then, looking around and noticing everyone's formal attire, Geo says, "How come they make ya wear a suit and tie, but they never check to see if there are excellent people underneath the clothing?"

There's a pianist in the corner, going up and down the scale like *Liberace,* which we both find far too theatrical for this mind-numbingly sedate situation. When I say, "I wish he'd find one note and just stick to it," Geo says, "Wouldn't it be funny if he was on an **acid trip** and nobody in the restaurant knew about it?"

Not that Geo isn't a connoisseur of fine dining. In fact, he says to the waitress,

"Ma'am, ma'am, nowhere on the menu do I see the word **'potato'."**

BABY OVEREATS

Then when the waitress explains that the salad is drizzled with fifty-year-old balsamic vinegar, he asks, "Nothing fresher than that?"

When the main course arrives, he perks up. I can tell because he takes a bite of his seared medallion of bison with eggless béarnaise sauce and says that it gives him a whole new outlook on life. . . ."Although," he adds, frowning, "the bread has a crust on it that's a job. Ya lose the calories ya gain trying to eat it."

Then, after annoying me by dumping a bottle of olive oil over the nice, clean white tablecloth, he says, **"THE LAST THING I WANT THIS TO BE IS A REALLY ANNOYIN' DINNERTIME."**

{ *By the way, if the fellow you're with tells you his scab is getting drier and that he's not gonna pick it off—he's gonna let it fall?—that's good news.* }

Then he adds, "There's a poppy seed stuck in my windpipe, and that last cough didn't help."

I like the way he uses the edge of the tablecloth as a napkin though. Very creative. I let him know, and even ask him, "What would you say the size of this table-cloth is?"

"In a parallel universe?" He says, helpfully . . . "Oh, it might be the size of six napkins—seven if its inhabitants are midgets."

As we finish the meal, and leave the nice restaurant, he says something that's so romantic, I'll never forget. "Tomorrow I have to go to the drugstore to get some more baby wipes. I use 'em to wipe my ass. Remind me."

How could I forget . . .

Hey Honey eyes—

The big baby went to the HOME-STYLE restaurant with the baby-baby, because she was pickin' up the check. But he ate too much—he had a plateful and he ate it just to be polite—also he felt intimidated by the esprit de corps the staff had. They were frightening—like a NR21 food cult. The next time the big baby eats there, he's going to wear his HITLER YOUTH uniform.

The bad man with the beard made SPOTTY stay out in the cold. But then he came out and gave Spotty two biscuits that help prevent loneliness when Sally's gone. George (who was sitting nearby) asked if he could have a few of the same biscuits. He misses Sally so.

I swear it all happened—

MR ABUNDANCE

The **Hamburger** Series

(stolen from Spot's files)

"This burger's so hard to chew, I think it might be meat from a cloned animal."

"Yeah, I think I remember eating this once before in a past lifetime . . . "

[ED. NOTE: THIS MEAL SUCKED. TOO GREASEY

What Geo taught Sal about **food**

GEORGE CARLIN'S
Kitchen and Food Tips

- The more stuff you put in the garbage disposal, the faster it sharpens the blade.

- Caramel sauce and ice cream should be eaten sans ice cream. You don't want the ice cream mucking up the caramel sauce.

- **One glass of wine for Sally, two for George.** But "one glass of wine" means it's filled to the rim—anything lower than the top line counts as half a glass.

- Eggs should be cooked evenly and all the way through.

- **The "beaver chomp."** The "beaver chomp" is when you take a mouthful of pasta, then chomp down and let everything that's hanging out of your mouth fall to the plate. It has to be a clean cut for the beaver chomp to be successful.

Demonstration of a failed beaver chomp.

TO THE EVER-CORDIALS,

THESE DOGS ARE NAMED SPRING, SUMMER, WINTER AND FALL. THEY ARE SAILING TO BELIZE TO OPEN A HOTEL WHICH THEY WILL NAME FOR THEMSELVES. IT WILL FEATURE FRENCH DOORS AND LOVELY BALCONIES. AND FREE CAPELLINI.
LOVE AND CANDLES from
- A BEAVER CHOMPER

SISTER SAL c/o WADE

MICHAEL SOWA "SEEMANNSLOS"
EDITION Inkognito · ERKELENZDAMM 11-13 · 1
5111

OH BOY, OH BOY — SALLY GOT A FREE CHOCOLATE DESSERT AT OLIVES.

"JOB SWITCHING" Originally Broadcast September 15, 1952

Sal says:

What happens in Vegas . . . shows up on the scale.

Sal, after polishing off the whole dessert tray at Olive's Restaurant in Las Vegas.

"Hey Sally, want some pudding?"

CHAPTER 15

We're Very Mature— For a Coupla Fuckin' Babies

HEY RESTAURANT LADY!

THE BIG BABY EATS A BIG BREAKFAST AND THEN ENJOYS DESSERT. HE SHOWS SALLY HIS BOWL TO EMPHASIZE HIS COMMITMENT TO CHOCOLATE. HE THEN BEGINS TO EXPLAIN HOW MUCH LOVE HE FEELS FOR BABY BABY: "GEEGLE OGGLE FLAGOOLYA GNIP." TRANSLATED LITERALLY, IT MEANS "DO YOU MIND IF I MOVE THIS CHAIR?" A LOOSER VERSION IS, "HOW THIS WOMAN MOVES MY SOUL AND REARRANGES MY CROTCH I WILL NEVER KNOW. I ONLY KNOW SHE HAS THE KEY TO MY HEART AND THE COMBINATION TO MY SOUL. I AM ALL HERS TILL THE FIRES GO OUT AND THE STARS FALL ASLEEP. HOW HAPPY I AM. WHAT A GREAT HEAVENLY PRIVELIGE IT IS TO BE IN HER LIFE AND TO HAVE HER SWEET VISAGE TO GAZE UPON." THE BIG BABY KNOWS HIS SHIT.

          GO LOVE ME,
          MR. FINE, THE MAN WHO LOVES

We're very mature —— for a coupla fuckin' babies.

Our combined Jupiterian ages (when no one's looking) are around seven or eight. I'm probably five—he's somewhere around three. In fact, you know how Crest toothpaste reads, "Warning! Keep out of reach of children under six years of age"? That's why we don't buy Crest; we use Colgate instead.

Hi Sarah!

I LOVE YOU.

LI'L GOOGIE

Hey there, you!

The baby is so
happy to be home.
He crosses his eyes.
His lips are ready
for a big kiss.

Hey Sally, you're the best!

Love eternal
The guy you light up
George

DO THE FROG HOP!

Do The
FROG
HOP!

We hop on the bed **a lot.**

In fact, that's the first thing we do whenever we get to another hotel. On our knees, holding hands. Not because we're having sex, but because we're playing frogs. Although Geo recommends holding "NUTS" and "TITS," so we don't end up in the ER from bouncing too much. We believe it wards off evil spirits. It doesn't matter if anybody believes that—it works for us. "And it's cheaper than Kabbalah water!" Geo adds.

By the way, **"Geo never tells Sal what to do, and everything he says is GOOD for the BOTH of us."** (He wrote that line. And told me to use it as often as possible, or at least whenever I talk about him.)

Hi. MY NAME IS "LITTLE GEOGIE." I AM SOLICITING DOLLAR BILLS SO I CAN BUY COOKIES FOR MY SWEET BABY ~~SARAH~~. SHE LOVES COOKIES, AND I LOVE HER. WON'T YOU PLEASE HELP A SMALL BOY IN LOVE?

Hi, SWEETER-THAN-THE-REST;
BOY, I LOVE YOU.
BOY, OH BOY, OH BOY!!
SORRY ABOUT THE GOOFY ALARM CLOCK.
B O-O-O-O! BOOO!
BOOOO ON THE CLOCK!
FUCK THE ROTTEN CLOCK.
HOORAY FOR US! YA-A-Y!
HALL-E-FUCKIN-LOO-YAH.
— YORE SOFTER PAL — GEORGIE BOY

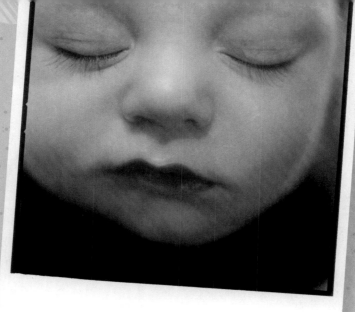

LITTLE BOY DREAMS

MISS MAGIC —

I HAVE BEEN COMPLETELY

SALLIFIED!!

— THE HANDSOME TROLL

TO PINK-NIPPLE WADE,

The beautiful boy dreams beautiful dreams of a beautiful girl. She is tall and blonde and slim and magnificently shaped. She is everything he would ever allow himself to wish for — and his wish comes true much later in his life. She appears, and sweeps him away with her enchanted and enchanting personality; her caring soul, and her love-filled heart.

from A FORMER LONER

I'M
SO
HAPPY

I'M LIKE
A
LITTLE
BOY

Hey COOKS—

This is an exclusive photo of the BIG BEEBEE as he quietly explains to the world the philosophy he and BEEBEE BEEBEE have devised as a way of life. He clever hand signal was flashed by the two whenever someone invited them over, or tried to include them in some group activity. They just wanted to be alone, so th could live their love.

Your ACE PAL,

CAKES

I THINK I SHIT.

LOVE TO Sara ~
Little
Georgia

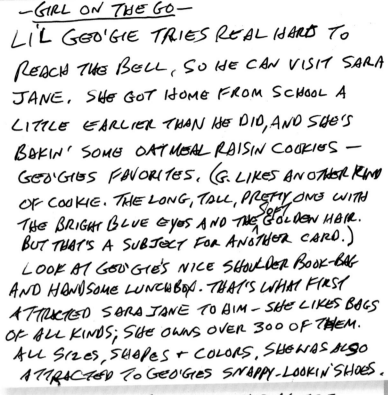

—GIRL ON THE GO—

LI'L GEO'GIE TRIES REAL HARD TO REACH THE BELL, SO HE CAN VISIT SARA JANE. SHE GOT HOME FROM SCHOOL A LITTLE EARLIER THAN HE DID, AND SHE'S BAKIN' SOME OATMEAL RAISIN COOKIES — GEO'GIES FAVORITES. (G. LIKES ANOTHER KIND OF COOKIE. THE LONG, TALL, PRETTY ONE WITH THE BRIGHT BLUE EYES AND THE SOFT GOLDEN HAIR. BUT THAT'S A SUBJECT FOR ANOTHER CARD.) LOOK AT GEO'GIE'S NICE SHOULDER BOOK-BAG AND HANDSOME LUNCHBOX. THAT'S WHAT FIRST ATTRACTED SARA JANE TO HIM — SHE LIKES BAGS OF ALL KINDS; SHE OWNS OVER 300 OF THEM. ALL SIZES, SHAPES + COLORS. SHE WAS ALSO ATTRACTED TO GEO'GIES SNAPPY-LOOKIN' SHOES.

THAT'S ANOTHER THING SARA HAS A LOT OF — SHOES. SHE HAS OVER 700 PAIRS. ALL SHAPES + STYLES + COLORS. BUT SHE'S DOIN' A REAL GOOD JOB OF KEEPIN' HER CLOSETS NEAT.

SARA IS A REAL GOOD GIRL!

AND GEO'GIE IS HEAD-OVER-HEELS IN LOVE WITH HER.

AFTER SCHOOL IS FUN.

LOVE + SMOOCHIES

— MAN ON THE RUN —

SARA JANE

BIG MAMA

I could ~~can~~ never

explain

how

much you

mean to

me.

PRETTY EYES
LOVES
PRETTY
EYES

I need you — and
I need you forever. BIG
BABY

MS SWEETNESS,

Many sweet roses
& match the many
ways I love you.
I marvel at your
prodigious capacity
for love and loving.

You are a sublime
dream that fills my
soul with light. SEÑOR
CUTIE-PIE

I DIDNT NEED ALL THIS
ART
SHIT.
THEY'RE FUCKING UP MY FORMAT.

ANYWAY .... MORE LOVE BACK HERE.
MR. MR.

LITTLE GEOGIE
LOVES
BABY SARAH
JANE

UH OH!
GEO'GIE FUCKED UP
AGAIN. SARA JANE
YELLED AT HIM, AND HE
BEGAN TO CRY. S.J. FELT
SO BAD SHE TRIED
TO CHEER HIM UP BY
SHOWIN' HIM HER
SNAPPER. A MINUTE LATER
HE WAS OKAY.
END OF TALE
THE ANONYMOUS CARD
MAN

THE "LITTLE GEOGIE" PHOTO SERIES—Ages 3 to 6

Somewhere around AGE 3
(he's coming out of his shell . . .)

AGE 4: He's beginning to hold a fork
and know what to do with it.

AGE 5, maybe?

AGE 6! Here he shows he can brush
his own teeth. That's as old as
he gets—in this chapter.

That's some **pitching arm . . .**

I once threw a bagel in a bagel lady's face
when she short-changed me ten dollars. She said I gave her a
ten-dollar bill when actually I'd given her a twenty. And after
arguing for a while, I got so frustrated, I threw a bagel in her
face. Afterward, Geo writes me this card . . .

BABY SARAH LOOKS BACK TO SEE IF LITTLE GEOGIE IS STILL WITH HER. SHE'S ON HER WAY TO THE STORE TO BUY A TOOTSIE ROLL, AND SHE WANTS HER LITTLE LOVER GUY TO BE THERE IN CASE SHE HAS TO THROW THE TOOTSIE ROLL BACK IN THE CLERK'S FACE LIKE THE INCIDENT AT ABBOT'S HABITS. SHOPPING ISN'T EASY FOR YOUNG SAL — IT'S A SERIES OF THROWING INCIDENTS.

Hey —
Come on out Baby Sarah;
There's nothing to be afraid
of. Honest.
Little Gingie and Big
Gingie ~~will~~ will make it safe
for you — we promise.
We love you both
very much
The Gingie Boys

SALLUS

Baby Sarah sleeps her gentle sleep
as dreams dance in and out of her
untroubled mind. Gergie sits nearby
protecting her from any outside influence that might disturb her serenity.
They take turns each night, keeping
watch over each other's peace of mind.
No two people before ever had such
a close and personal coexistence.
Their BABY love is fully mature.

MR GOOSKI

Cooks —
When I open
the door to my heart,
this is what I see:
Little Sarah Jane lookin'
at a flower. You are
my powerful engine of
love — INNOCENT + SEXY.
BIG GEO'GIE

WHO IS THIS MAN ? ? ?

Hey ~~Slow~~ Hey Slim —

Georg (a slightly older big baby) finally figures out the central theme of his HBO show.

He loves his Sally,
He loves his bubble,
He loves his life now.
WoW!

Georgie Boy

AS, HAND IN HAND, THESE TWO CUTE RASCALS PROCEED DOWN THE ROAD OF LIFE TO-GETHER, THEY ENCOUNTER ELEMENTS AND ASPECTS OF LIFE THAT TAKE THEM BY SURPRISE AND SOMETIMES ANGER OR SCARE THEM. BY HOLD-ING HANDS AND SHARING HEARTS THEY ALWAYS MANAGE TO MAKE THINGS A LITTLE BETTER — AND A LITTLE EASIER NEXT TIME. THEIR LIVES ARE A PROCESS OF RISKING AND GROWING. RISKING THE SAFETY THEY FEEL AT THE MOMENT, ON A CHANCE TO GROW EVEN MORE FULFILLED AT A LATER TIME. AND ON THEY GO — BEING REASSURED AND TAKING CHANCES NITE AFTER NITE UNTIL THE FILM OF THE AFTERNOON

HEY COOKIE, COMES AROUND AND MAKES THEM PROUD AND WELL.

LOVE DR. BOOKGE

GEORGE + SARAH HANSEN & CO.

TWO OF A KIND —

IN SEPERABLE !

The love of your life —
Lyle

CHAPTER 16

Goofy Stuff

Be a tree!

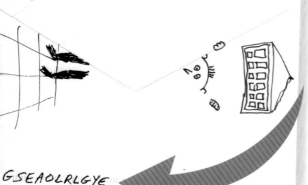

YOU'RE MY LIFE'S BIG WOW!

Geo with a mutual feeling

GSEAOLRLGYE

Gseaolrlgye.

As soon as Geo walked off-stage, he became who he really was: the finest person I've ever known.

One day, Geo said to me, "I may possibly be the finest person I've ever known. I'm still checking a few names, but it's looking more and more like I'm the one."

I said, "That's true, Geo. As long as you don't take Sal into account."

Geo says, "That's a given, Sally Wade. In fact, you're so sharp, you'd make a razor blade walk away in shame."

He liked the way he phrased that. He liked the way he phrased most everything. SO DID I.

And when I told him that, he said, "The feeling is mutual."

GEORGE CARLIN WAS ALL ABOUT THE INDIVIDUAL.

And although he claims not to "sacrifice my individuality for the sake of the group"—and that it's "diluted thinking"—he turns George and Sally's names into one person . . .

Geo writes notes about how much alike we are becoming—and thinks it's great when I'm more like him. He even makes it sound like his way is the right way to begin with.

I'M GETTIN' MORE SPONTANEOUS & SALLY IS NAILIN' THINGS DOWN.

I'm cutting down my TV Time & Sally is increasing hers.

MORE BLENDING OF THE JUPITER TWINS' IDENTITIES

Once, during a radio interview, Geo explains our relationship to the host by saying, "It was like a **THUNDERBOLT.** Sally enjoys the destruction of mankind as much as I do!"

The host said, "That's great. At least you have a partner, someone to share it with!"

I was listening to the radio at the time, and found it so romantic, I fell in love all over again.

SAL + GEO

"MICRO"
&
"MACRO"
went out to play —
and said, "Oh Boy,
Oh Boy. It's another
great day."

UP WE GO

DOWN WE GO

Hey,
ESSEE
What I'M BRINGIN' out
in in YOUR MALE
And what you're bringin'
out in ME is my FEMALE!

THAT'S THE MAGIC !

My male, you female
My female, you male

A CLUSTER-FUCK !!

LISTEN, MISSY SALLY !
YOU DIDN'T THINK
I WOULD OVER-
LOOK THIS AS A
GOOD LOCATION FOR
ANOTHER — STILL
ANOTHER — "I
LOVE
YOU"!!
DID YOU? SHAME!
LOVER GEORGE

Although I hate to blow anybody's illusions, Geo was worried about Y2K. He stayed up all night in Vegas, staring at the computer, waiting for it to crash. The next morning, when he was disappointed because nothing had happened, I said, "Geo'gie, I'm really sorry the Y2K catastrophe didn't happen and the banks weren't wiped out. Maybe something bigger will happen, maybe a meteor will hit. Maybe Ebola will break out. Or Listeria, Salmonella, or Encephalitis. And remember, at any moment, millions of asteroids are crossing the orbit of Earth."

"Yeah," he says. "Impacts will happen. It's just a matter of time. Maybe we'll get lucky!"

Then he adds, "Speaking of lucky . . . I had **Ebola** and **AIDS** at the same time and they ate each other up."

 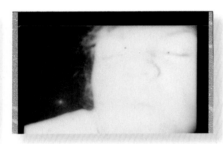

A couple of bookends: photos Geo & Sal take of each other, while waiting all night for Y2K

Geo seemed ordinary at times.

He was ordinary at times. While riding in the car, I notice I'm with the type of guy who shouts, "YOUSA!" whenever there's a lull in the conversation. For no apparent reason! So I try not to lull.

Also, he's a two-footed driver, just like he's a two-finger typist. In fact, he drives like a little old lady—with one foot on the gas and another foot on the brake. So we're either goin' ninety-five miles per hour—just whizzin' along—or we aren't movin' at all—because we just hit a brick wall.

There's no *lag* time—you just go straight through the windshield. Oh, to hear Spot tell it—he ended up on the sidewalk dozens of times and then in the ER getting x-rayed for whiplash.

OH MY GOD!!

THE PHANTOM NOTE-
LEAVER STRIKES
YET ONE MORE TIME.

EYE - A
OVE - LAY
OO - YAY.
YES HE DO.
ALL MY SWEETNESS,
GEORGE

WOOF!

TONGUE

PIG DOG!!

And he doesn't think pedestrians should have the right of way; so if one crosses his path, he keeps going without slowing down. And if anyone complains about the fact that his car is in the crosswalk, Geo lowers the window and shouts, "Let me get this straight. In order to get around the city, you require drivers to stop for you?" And then he peels out.

Did Geo mind if Sal drove?

Well, he hated being a passenger and couldn't quite get the seat adjusted to his fit and suddenly acted like he had a bad back. In fact, that's the only time he never said anything. He just kind of moaned and grimaced and rubbed the back of his shoulders. Eventually, we settled on Spot driving so he'd quit squirming.

WHAT I LEARNED ABOUT PERFORMING FROM GEO:

One night I ask him, "What do you do if you have to fart on stage?"

He says, "If you have to fart onstage? Wait for a big laugh."

So I say, "And if they're not laughing?"

"If they're not laughing, say something like, 'I was waiting for a laugh to fart. So far? No opportunity. Now might be a good time!'"

DOES SPOT KNOW ABOUT THIS?

. . . About including Spot's sobriety classes in this book . . .

Spot drives Geo and Sal to PETCO, before and after his sobriety classes.

PERFECTION
IS THE
ENEMY
OF GOOD.

Fortunately, both Jupiter Geo and Sal are advocates of **huge natural disasters** with Mother Nature succeeding, of course. Otherwise, that might've been a deal breaker. In fact, Geo keeps a record of deadly quakes; and has lists of earthquake death totals dating back to 1976.

"But," he qualifies, "some of these death totals are very disappointing. Except one in Tangshan, China, in 1976 when in an 8.2 earthquake 240,000 were killed—now that's a worthwhile earthquake! If something like that was centered under L.A. or San Francisco, you might get close to having some decent numbers. Otherwise, like the one in southeast Turkey in 2003, a 6.4 magnitude quake and only 167 people were killed . . . Why bother mentioning it?" he explains to Sal, who says, "I see what you're talkin' about. Unless you are 168. Then you might want to point it out."

In fact, whenever they say on the news, "This is a warning, the following tape contains pictures that are extremely graphic," unless it relates to animals—in which case we'd immediately change the channel—we stop whatever we're doing and pull our chairs closer to the screen.

"Everything is rigged, slanted, distorted, hyped, exaggerated, overstated, and falsified. No one cares about Jackie O's nipple rings," Geo says.

"Except us," I say.

"And why do these news anchors all look like they have an eight-foot tempered-steel rod sticking up their hind quarters?" Spot says. Then after a few moments of silence, we hear the cork pop on Spot's wine. A nice bottle of chardonnay. And I whisper to George, "An eight-foot tempered-steel rod? . . . Maybe you should stop talking around the dog."

"Oh, I don't know," Geo says, as he takes the glass of wine Spot offers. "I think he's a good boy."

Here's something Geo wouldn't want anyone to tell about him . . . **except me.** (That's because nobody knows about it except me.) He cut his last show short, at the L.A. amphitheater, so that he could rush home to see the season finale of *Desperate Housewives*. (We were in a rental house with no TiVo, while our house was getting fixed.) He always rushed home to be with me anyway, but he *really* rushed home for that. In fact, he's so excited about knowing something that Spot (a connoisseur of pop culture) and I don't know— *which is that one of the regulars is going to get knocked off*—that he leaves the stage ten minutes early. It's a secret he now says he wants me to share—and since the show has already aired, he won't be giving anything away.

By the way, when Spot asked him which part of his act he left out to make it home on time, and Geo said, "The middle!"

Spot rolled over and played dead.

And not just for a treat, he was hoping no one would recognize him the next time he left the house. He has a reputation to uphold.

My step-dad is NOT George Carlin. I never even met him! Well, maybe once . . .

TIVO TRAUMA

I am the TiVo expert. Geo doesn't understand TiVo. (In all fairness, it's very difficult for a Jupiterian to grasp the concept of moving forward and backward in time—since we feel we're everywhere at once.) He would call from Vegas and when I offer advice, he asks, "Now, will that back up the sports show from the beginning? I don't wanna miss the ending." And in Vegas at his condo, instead of a hooker's phone number on the nightstand, I notice he keeps a TiVo expert's phone number, in case he gets stuck.

"You're recording something in real time. How does that work? What if you wanna move ahead in future time?"

"You need a TiVo Time Machine for that," I say.

"Only on this planet," he adds. *"On* JUPITER, *you don't."*

Also, Geo talks all the way through any American or British murder mystery, to try and figure out the ending as soon as it begins. He says, "Is he setting us up?"

"What?" I ask.

Which interrupts the next scene, and when I back it up, he asks something else—"Do you think that guy did it? What could his motivation be? He looks suspicious to me, doesn't he? Or maybe it's that lady he screwed. Hmm . . . who do ya think the murderer is gonna be?" Then he'll try to compliment me—"Well, you're the screenwriter, so you know how these plots work better than I do."

This annoying habit, Spot believes, stemmed from his childhood. Hating ambiguity was a long-standing issue of Geo's—because his father wasn't around—and his mother was never home. (Just like Spot's!) That's what Spot says Geo's shrink said once, which he claims gives Geo (the two of them, actually) the moral authority to pause the TiVo and back up the program, over and over again, often enough to turn a one- or two-hour program into a three or four-hour ordeal, while examining each clue and plot point, even if they turn out to be dead ends.

"See what not having the right upbringing will do to ya?" Spot says to me, pointedly.

GEO: I may not know everything, but I'm closing in on it.

SAL: You know, you almost have the same initials as Jesus Christ? You only missed it by one letter.

HA HA HA HA HA HA
HEE HEE HEE HEE
HO HO HO HO HO
WOW!   ME LOVE YOU

WHAT OTHER WORD DO YOU GET IF YOU REARRANGE THE LETTERS G-E-O? E-G-O.

That's what **he** had—a big, positive, handsome, charming, lovable, sexy, smart, empowering ego—that was always on my side as well as his own. In fact, when Geo gets home from the road, he says he's "gotta practice bein' a real person again." So, he walks around the room, shakes his own hand, and says to himself, "What a fine gentleman I am!"

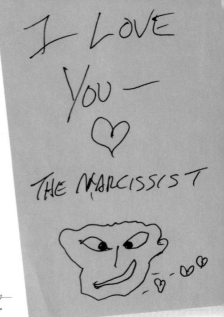

HE KNOWS HE HAS CUTE LEGS TOO.

Even his mother told him so. Absolutely perfect. Like a teenager's legs. *Fabulous knees, nice ankles, decent enough feet.* In fact, if you were to tell Geo that you thought his legs looked great, he'd stretch one of them up in the air and admire its greatness all over again. You couldn't compliment Geo's legs too often.

"Absolutely perfect," I'd say, agreeing with his mother.

"LOVE ME, LOVE MY LIVER SPOTS"

Don't worry, **Chick-a-Lito,** when you have power, success, and good looks, people are gonna talk.

~ FOWL MOUTH

HE MICROMANAGES KLEENEXES.

Geo doesn't want to loan me too many Kleenexes from his stash, because without someone being as careful as he is, his supply will quickly dwindle. That's the logic. So in New York, when the air is cold and my nose is runny, he carefully peels off two or three from a roll, hands them to me before I go outside, and says, "Out of those, just **use what you need.**"

AS FOR TOILET PAPER . . .

One time, in the middle of the night, when I hear something downstairs, and I ask him if he knows what it is, he says, "Most noises are not anything." Instead of going downstairs to investigate.

"Most noises are not anything," . . . I repeat to myself. In fact, it's the kind of observation that makes you say, "Hmmm . . . that's true!" Instead of, "Why don't you go downstairs and find out?" By then, burglars could've hauled off anything—such as the bargain-size package of toilet paper in the garage. That's what they took the last time. I thought it was odd that someone would take that and not the extra microwave, but Geo could see why. From a male point of view.

HERE'S ANOTHER GOOFY THING

Geo codes the word "**sex**" in his journals, in case the FBI confiscates them. In fact, every time we have sex, he marks it in such a way that he thinks would make it really difficult for the CIA computer experts to crack the code: with a big red X. He says he wants to keep our lovemaking a secret from "Big Brother," because he doesn't want the world to know what a good thing he has.

Geo buys walkie-talkies so we can walk down the alley together in front of our house without losing contact. For some reason, we can hear each other better in person, but not over the walkie-talkies. "Maybe they need batteries," I say to him. And, when we go in separate directions at the end of the block—unlike a cell phone where you can still hear each other around the world. Once we are out of range and the signal is dropped, we have to *shout* about our love. Actually, we only used them once, because they were kind of heavy and didn't work, so after that, Geo stuck them in the back of a drawer.

"It was a good idea at the time though, and I'm glad we tried them out," I said to him afterward.

"Me too," he says.

"Otherwise, we'd have always wondered about the range of our love on walkie-talkies."

I think he bought 'em at Toys R Us, but since ours weren't very powerful, if you're in the market for walkie-talkies, I'd try Radio Shack. "A true 'fak,'" as he'd say.

Later we record our top secret conversation on paper.

"Anything that feels this good is in danger of being made illegal in this society."

> SISTER SILK—
>
> I'm not going to tell anyone else about how much I love you and how happy you make me, because I'm afraid the word will get around, and they'll make it illegal.
>
> Anything that feels this good is in danger of being made illegal in this society.
>
> I LOVE YOU !!
>
> YOU BITCH!
>
> LOVE FROM YOUR OTHER HALF

> Hi Hi, Hi-Hi!
> YOU SO SWEET.
> BYE BYE,
> PIE-PIE

> Pie pie,
> You so sweeter.
> Bye Bye,
> Hi Hi.

The ink will become invisible over time, but it's fine now.

Goofy
notes

LOOK! SALLY & SPOT
ON THE BEACH, CLEAR-
ING THEIR HEADS.
GEORGE FISHES NEARBY.
SALLY'S BONNET IS NEW,
BUT SHE'S HAD THE BELT
FOR SOME TIME NOW.
GEORGE LOVES HER.
HE WILL BE ARRESTED
SOON.   LOVE,
THE MODEL GUY

Mr. Sally Wade

Do you love
me As much (check here) ☐
or MORE (check here) ✓
than I
love you?

GUESS who I
Still love?
check one

GEO ☒

NIXON ☐

The way we end our conversations:

GEO TO SAL:
Gimme a kiss, Goofy.

SAL TO GEO:
Gimme a kiss, Goofy.

You
STILL
LOVE
ME?

You
STILL
LOVE
ME?
Not the SAME
Amount. Much more

YES   ☑ FUCK YES

SALLY,

NEW YORK IS SHROUDED IN MYSTERY AS AN IMPENDING TRIP EAST BY N.Y.'S FAVORITE LOVE COUPLE IS ANNOUNCED BY LIZ SMITH IN HER NEWSDAY COLUMN. FIFTH AVENUE IS BEING SPRUCED UP; CENTRAL PARK IS BEING VACUUMED; THE HUDSON RIVER IS BEING FILTERED AND THE GEORGE WASHINGTON BRIDGE IS BEING DECLARED A SACRED PLACE IN HONOR OF "THE BRIDGE OVER THE CANAL" WHERE SAL + GEO FIRST PAUSED TO TAKE A FEW STEPS INTO THEIR LOVE STATE.

YOUR STORYTELLER, GEORGE

CHAPTER 17

Snapshots from New York

I'M NOT IN A FOG — ITS CLEAR ... I LOVE YOU

New York is our "home-away-from-home," where Geo goes to do most of his HBO shows and Sal gets her hair done. (Of equal importance in our Jupiterian lives, leaning more toward hair.)

As Sal once explains to Geo, "The way women feel about a good **blow-dry,** is the same way men feel about a good **blow job**. Perks ya up. Makes you feel good about yourself. Raises your confidence and self-esteem. Keeps it from sticking out all over."

Outside on the sidewalk, in front of the Beacon Theatre, videos of the *You Are All Diseased* show are playing over a loudspeaker.

Geo walks past his display,
so Sal can take a picture.

A JUPITEREAN TAXI RUSHES

TO THOSE WHO CARE A LOT—

TAXI, NEW YORK NIGHT, 1947-48
PHOTOGRAPH BY TED CRONER

JUPITER ACCOUNT OF G+S BEHAVIOR —
THE CRAZY COUPLE HAS ZOOMED
AROUND TOWN SINCE JAN. 26TH,
COMING AND GOING LIKE TWO
MAD GEESE — RIDING FROM REST-
AURANT TO RESTAURANT AND STUDIO
TO STUDIO IN THEIR SPECIAL
24-CYLINDER, BRUSHED STAINLESS-
STEEL TAXI CAB, KISSING LIKE
PROM KIDS IN THE BACK SEAT
WITH CONDOMS AND POT. IT'S LOVE.
IT'S LOVE
IT'S LOVE

© TED CRONER. COURTESY HOWARD GREENBERG GALLERY, NEW YORK
© FOTOFOLIO, BOX 661 CANAL STA., NY, NY 10013
F385   ISBN 1-881270-62-9

GEORGE + SALLY TO THEIR
HOTEL FOLLOWING THE HBO SHO

NYC

Here I am in love
Here I am in New York City —
   where my heartbeat started.
Here it continues in the hands
   of Sally Wade :

Sally snuggled and ramped me
   openly on the plane. Sally shows
me her love all the time. Sally
   is my girl.

I've never felt so open — so at ease;
I've never felt this joy and peace;
I've never fallen so deeply —
I never had Sally Wade.

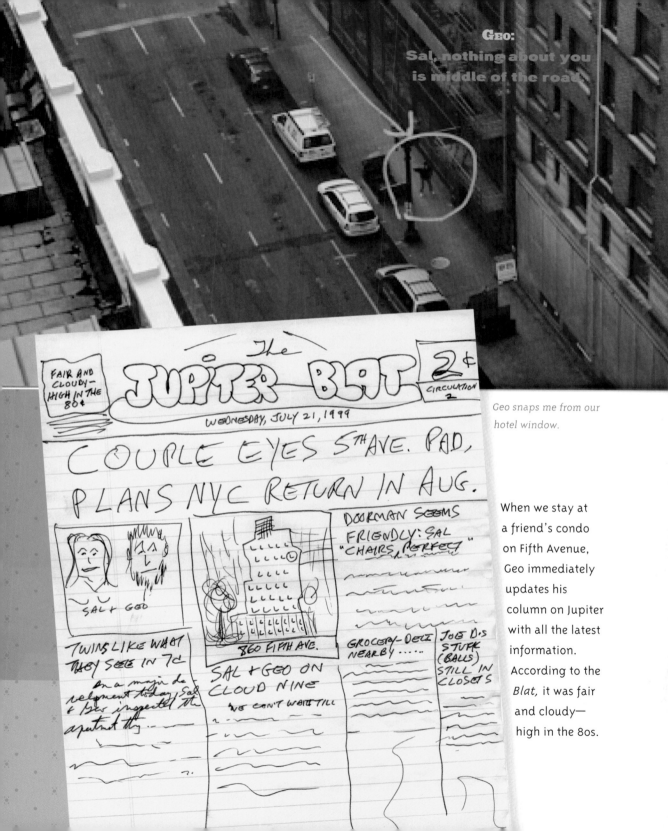

GEO:

Sal, nothing about you is middle of the road.

Geo snaps me from our hotel window.

FAIR AND CLOUDY— HIGH IN THE 80s

The JUPITER BLAT

2¢

CIRCULATION 2

WEDNESDAY, JULY 21, 1999

COUPLE EYES 5TH AVE. PAD, PLANS NYC RETURN IN AUG.

SAL + GEO

TWINS LIKE WHAT THEY SEE IN 7C

860 FIFTH AVE.

SAL + GEO ON CLOUD NINE

WE CAN'T WAIT TILL

DOORMAN SEEMS FRIENDLY: SAL "CHAIRS, PERFECT"

GROCERY-DELI NEARBY ......

JOE D.'S STUFF (BALLS) STILL IN CLOSETS

When we stay at a friend's condo on Fifth Avenue, Geo immediately updates his column on Jupiter with all the latest information. According to the *Blat,* it was fair and cloudy— high in the 80s.

The Fifth Avenue Dog Gang is all excited, because they heard that Spot Wade was moving to New York City and they wanted to show him where all the good smells are. They didn't know that Sal & Geo decided to leave Spot with Gene Jack and Clanya and Clanya's children, while they came East to make love in their new place on Fifth Avenue. Even though they were disappointed, they told Sal & Geo they were welcome to New York and then they each took a dump. I really do love you, Sally — George

SAL & GEO GO SHOPPING ON FIFTH AVENUE

At Saks Fifth Avenue, I notice it's easy for men to shop. There aren't as many choices for men as there are for women. Here's what Geo says to the sales-lady there:

"I'll take a sweater in **dark grey, dark silver,** or **black.** Make it come in around two or three hundred dollars. If it's any cheaper than that, it's not gonna be any good. **Nothing that scratches like a bastard.** Plain is good. Unadorned. **We don't want no fancy stitches that suggest a designer's ego is involved, jackin' up the prices."**

SAL DRESSES UP FOR GEO, BUT NOT FOR THE USUAL REASONS.

I dress as a foil, a cover-up, to counterbalance whatever he's wearing. We're on a secret reconnaissance mission to fool people into thinking he's dressed up too. That way, if I walk in ahead of him at a nice restaurant, we figure no one will notice that he has on a fleece jacket and New Balance tennis shoes.

Geo dresses for Sal too, as you can see from this note.

When I point out the obvious—which is that they emphasize his great legs—he's overjoyed.

THE FIRST PENNY APPEARS AS WE HEAD TOWARD THE TRAFFIC— IT WAS ANOTHER "GREAT FIND" for EAGLE-EYE CARLIN.

GEO'GIE BOUGHT SOME EASTER PANTS ! ! !

MORE WALKING

Supervised by Jupiter, they land at Barney's for makeup and underwear.

More walking — supervised by Jupiter at 72ND + Madison — and they land at Barneys for MAKEUP and UNDERWEAR. Sally gets some of what she needs — Geo decides to EXPER IMENT WITH JOCKEY SHORTS!!

Sally bought two outfits — one was really great and the other one is going back tomorrow. But she's keeping the SCRATCHY BLUE NIGHTIE ENSEMBLE.

Sal has **two looks.**

"Jeans, a nice jacket, and boots, or the same baggy-ass jogging pants I slept in the night before." I tell Geo that on our first date, and he remembers and writes me this card:

HEY, LEGS!

GEORGE GETS ALL TANKED UP ON DIET COKE AND HAS A BAD DREAM: THAT SWEET SALLY VISITS NEIMAN-MARCUS AND IS TALKED INTO HAVING A TOTAL MAKEOVER, INCLUDING TOO MUCH JEWELRY, TOO-BIG GLOVES AND A BIRD THAT FLEW INTO HER HEAD AND LODGED THERE. WHEN GEORGE WOKE UP, HE WAS REZIEVED TO SEE SALLY NEXT TO HIM IN HER BAGGY-ASS JOGGING PANTS AND NEW YORK SWEATSHIRT. ROLLED OVER AND HUGGED HIMSELF AFTER GIVING SALLY A BIG KISS. —YO'GUY

C/O WADE
SWEET GIRL A
MY DREEMS
NAL

MON

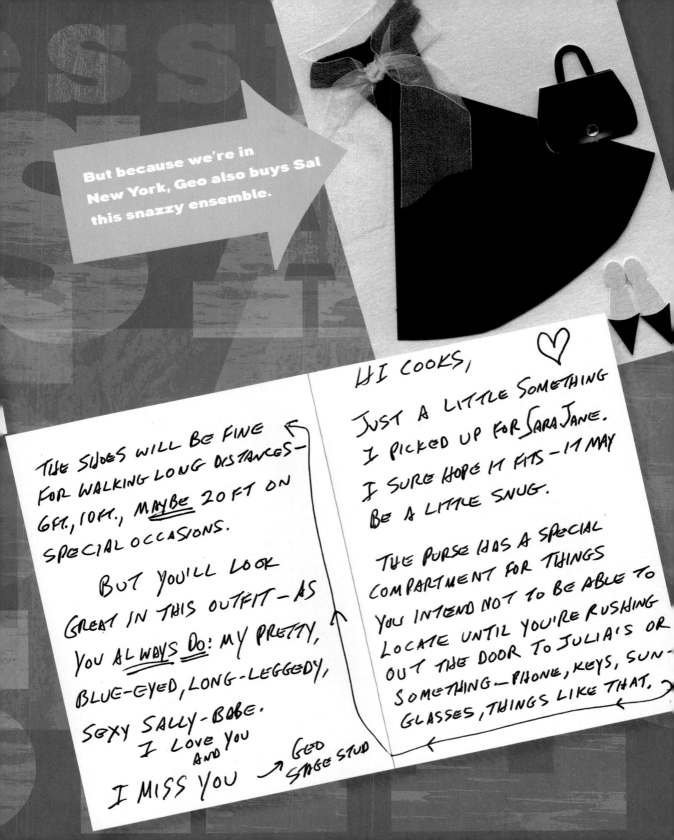

But because we're in New York, Geo also buys Sal this snazzy ensemble.

THE SHOES WILL BE FINE FOR WALKING LONG DISTANCES— 6FT., 10FT., MAYBE 20FT ON SPECIAL OCCASIONS.

BUT YOU'LL LOOK GREAT IN THIS OUTFIT—AS YOU ALWAYS DO: MY PRETTY, BLUE-EYED, LONG-LEGGEDY, SEXY SALLY-BABE.
I LOVE YOU AND YOU
I MISS YOU → GEO STAGE STUD

HI COOKS, ♡

JUST A LITTLE SOMETHING I PICKED UP FOR Sara Jane. I SURE HOPE IT FITS—IT MAY BE A LITTLE SNUG.

THE PURSE HAS A SPECIAL COMPARTMENT FOR THINGS YOU INTEND NOT TO BE ABLE TO LOCATE UNTIL YOU'RE RUSHING OUT THE DOOR TO JULIA'S OR SOMETHING—PHONE, KEYS, SUN-GLASSES, THINGS LIKE THAT.

ON A TOUR GEO GIVES SAL

At Riverside Park and 72nd Street, we yell, "I love you," in the tunnel. Later, Sal suggests that they buy bacon, eggs, and bread for a homeless guy on the sidewalk. When we hand him the grocery bag, the homeless guy looks inside and is angry that it doesn't contain booze, so Geo slips him another hundred.

RIVERSIDE PARK AND 72ND STREET. WE EACH YELLED "I LOVE YOU" IN THE TUNNEL — ALTHOUGH SALLY WAS RELUCTANT. SALLY PEED IN THE COMFORT STATION and we STOOD AND STARED AT THE HUDSON RIVER "SHIT LINE." TAXI BACK TO HOTEL FOR HAIRCUTS — MARK WAS LATE. GEO. WENT FOR A TURKEY SANDWICH FOR SALLY — IT WAS GOOD.

WE DECIDED "FUCK THE HALLOWEEN PARADE" * AND WALKED UPTOWN TO LUSARDI'S. WE BOUGHT BACON, EGGS and BREAD for A HOMELESS GUY. SIX TEENAGE GIRLS REALLY PISSED SALLY OFF WHEN THEY SAID "GEORGE!"

We stay up all night, playing with **puppets.** We buy them on the streets of New York, and create untoward characters.

official sleep night *

* THE NIGHT WE GOT ALMOST NO SLEEP

GEO. WAS REFERRED TO AS AN "ASS WIPE," BY THE PUPPET.

BALLY'S
LAS VEGAS
25th Anniversary

Geo completes his TO-DO LIST

.... will conquer everything. In our case its true. Especially if we moved to the Ozarks. I'd have an initial adjustment period — but, on balance, I'd make a pretty good hick. I got the accent already — all I need is to let my teeth go. STICK WITH ME, AND I'LL PUT YOU ON BROADWAY .... →

SALLY GIRL —

I'll bet you look beautiful — as USUAL!!

I got a spare room key —
I went to KINKOS & got the HBO documents printed.
I put the film in to be developed.
I got 2 hot dogs.
I found a nearby place with KALIBER.

I ALSO FOUND A DIME.

I found a possible substitute place NEARBY for when the BREAD PEOPLE are closed after 3 PM.
I did EVERYTHING! I'M SO GOOD!!!!

Love from the bottom of my pants — Your guy — Geo

... PICKING UP CHANGE. LOVE EVER GEO

$2.00

...teurs et G. Le Scanff, J.C. Mayer 1998
...fset printed in France / ED 154

7 64697 00116

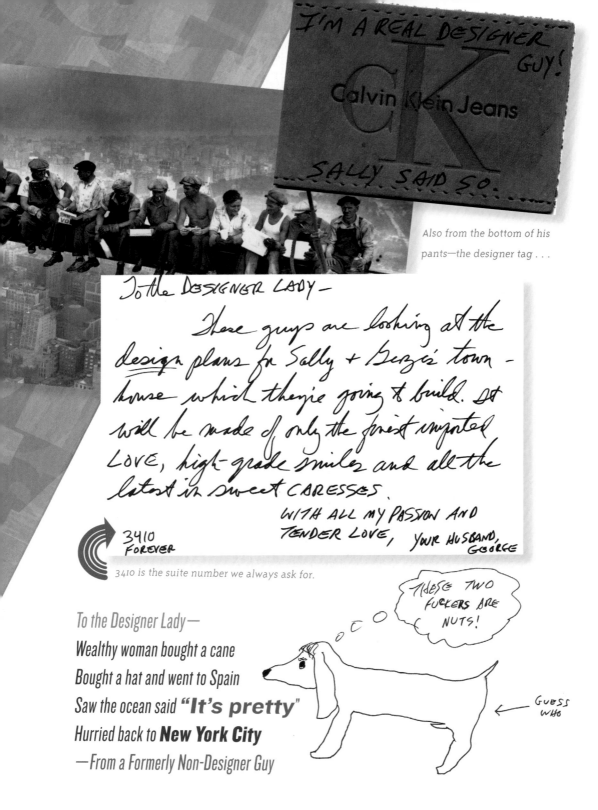

I'M A REAL DESIGNER GUY!

Calvin Klein Jeans

CK

SALLY SAID SO.

Also from the bottom of his
pants—the designer tag . . .

To the DESIGNER LADY—

These guys are looking at the design plans for Sally + Berg's town-house which they're going to build. It will be made of only the finest imported LOVE, high-grade smiles and all the latest in sweet CARESSES.

WITH ALL MY PASSION AND TENDER LOVE, YOUR HUSBAND, GEORGE

3410 FOREVER

3410 is the suite number we always ask for.

THESE TWO FUCKERS ARE NUTS!

GUESS WHO

To the Designer Lady—

Wealthy woman bought a cane
Bought a hat and went to Spain
Saw the ocean said "It's pretty"
Hurried back to **New York City**
—From a Formerly Non-Designer Guy

THE MEDIA IN NEW YORK

There are certain shows Geo likes doing, such as Letterman, Jon Stewart, Keith Olbermann, and others.

Imus is another one he has fun with . . . especially when Geo and Imus agree that Sal is right on *Imus in the Morning*. In fact, Geo brings home the following transcript to prove it to Sal.

Sal photographs Geo on the hotel room TV on *Countdown with Keith Olbermann*

IMUS: Your take on George Bush?

GEO: Well, here's a man whose biggest ambition is to take a nap. I said to Sally, I said, the man— he's obviously a man with no . . .

IMUS: Who is Sally?

GEO: Sally is the woman in my life the last three years. We're stupendously in love. We live on Jupiter, you might say.

IMUS: Good for you.

GEO: But I said to Sally, George Bush is a man with no discernible gifts. And she said, "It's never stopped any of these people before and so he's right in the mold."

IMUS: And she's right too, by the way!

"See?" Geo says, after he reads it to Sal. "We both agree you were right."

SLIM

A WOMAN OVERCOME WITH EMOTION CONCERNING GEORGE AND SALLY'S LOVE AFFAIR ATTEMPTS TO FLY TO JUPITER. SHE FAILS. INSTEAD SHE FLIES TO BROOKLYN WHERE SEXUAL MAN SHE MEETS THE LOVE OF HER LIFE.

MY HOPE AND GLORY

ACTION SHOTS

We call all blurry photos "Jupiterian," and are required to send the negatives to Jupiter, where they keep them on file, as further evidence that this planet is crazy.

On the sidewalk in New York, we found this, written in stone.

CHAPTER 16

Drug Stuff

SARAH,
WHAT YOU CAN'T SEE
IS ME UP ON THE MOUN-
TAIN. I'M SHOUTING TO
THE WORLD ABOUT MY LOVE TO
FOR SALLY WADE — AND
THEY'RE GOING TO PUT ME
TO SLEEP, BECAUSE I'M
KEEPING OTHER PEOPLE
AWAKE. THEY JUST
DON'T UNDERSTAND HOW
MUCH I LOVE YOU.
DENIS

TO THE GIRL WHO LIVES
IN MY HEART

FROM THE MAN WHO SLEEPS
IN HER DREAMS

U.S.A., WORLD, MILKY WAY

668
AMAZING COLOSSAL MAN © ORION PICTURES
© THE AMERICAN POSTCARD CO. INC. NYC
ALL RIGHTS RESERVED PRINTED IN USA

He signs his middle name, "Denis"

Well, this chapter is going to be disappointing

to any druggie who reads it, because eight or nine months into the relationship, I say to Geo, "About that funny-smelling cigarette stuff . . ." And he says, "Okay, you want me to stop using it?" I say, "Yeah, I'd appreciate that," and he never touched weed again. And I think that's why.

Then, a few months later, I say, "Those three beers you and Spot share in the afternoon?"

"Out?" he asks.

"Right on," I say.

"Yo, dude!" Spot says to Geo. "Traitor!"

This is where drugs come into play . . . Oh, not the "hippie dippy" stuff—I'm talking prescription meds. In fact, any medication sold over the counter was fair game to Geo. Meaning? He took a lot of unnecessary drugs.

For example, one day we're in the grocery store, counting how many items have to do with kitty litter for a piece he's writing. And I'm about to tell him why Scott toilet paper (my preference) is preferable to Charmin (his choice)—obviously, because there are more tissues per roll than any other brand, in spite of Charmin being softer—and he says to me, "Hang on a sec. I need to take some Tylenol." When I ask, "Why?" he says, "Because I think I might be getting a headache."

"Don't you want to find out first?" I ask.

"No, because by then it'll be too late."

"But if you don't get a headache . . . ?"

"I'm still in the clear because I've taken Tylenol. . . .When did Noah build the ark?" he asks. "*Before* the rain."

Another example, we're lying in bed one night, and we hear a commercial that says, "Men, are you urinating more frequently? Do you wake up at night to urinate? If so, you need Flomax, medicine for frequent nighttime urination!"

I say, "Who'd be gullible enough to buy that?" and chuckle.

He stares straight ahead and says nothing. So I'm suspicious enough to get up and go into the bathroom, open the medicine cabinet, and lo and behold, there it is on the top shelf: "Flomax, nighttime frequent urination medicine." Apparently, he'd already seen that commercial.

Then we hear another commercial: "Ladies? Are your drains stopped up? If so, then you need Liquid-Plumr!" When I pause the TV, I notice the same nonchalant gaze on Geo's face that he had when watching the Flomax ad. So I go back into the bathroom, open the cabinet beneath the sink, find the Liquid-Plumr, then return and answer the announcer: "Nope, we're all set here, but thanks for the tip!"

The next commercial is for Requip, to combat "restless leg syndrome." When Geo rearranges himself into a noticeably relaxed position, I don't bother to check the medicine cabinet. I know it's in there.

GEO TO PEOPLE IN LINE AT THE PHARMACY:

"I don't personally take drugs anymore, but that doesn't mean I don't recommend it to other people."

ABOUT DRINKING

Believe it or not, although I've never seen Geo act drunk, I know he can overindulge. So we have a rule about drinking: he could have two glasses of wine, three times a week—that was our rule—whereas my limit is one glass, three times a week. (I don't need a rule, but Geo likes rules, and I want to be fair.) The problem is, in most restaurants, what they consider one drink is what we call "half a glass." It has to be to the top of the rim or else it's not one glass by our standards. It's "half a glass." So sometimes, we order two glasses to get one drink. That's our system. In case anyone wants to copy it, it's yours for the taking.

THANG KYOO!

Did it work? No.

When Geo decides to stop drinking, he says, "Okay, I'll only drink O'Doul's." O'Doul's is a fake, non-alcoholic beer with 0.1 percent alcohol. So if you drink ten or twenty of them, like he does, you can get the alcohol content of maybe one beer. He did this for about a day and a half, then gave those up too. No one's that thirsty.

But that doesn't mean he isn't the cutest thing to ever set foot on this planet in my opinion, and I tell him as much.

And then one day, we're in New York, and I notice Geo is taking **Vicodin**, which I knew about (although not the dosage), and Ambien, which I had no idea was addictive. Then he announces that he's going out to lunch at one of our favorite places by himself, which he's never done before. My instinctive antenna goes up, and I suspect it's for a glass of wine. Bothered enough to not be able to sleep that night, and realizing things may be spiraling out of control for him, I write him a note, asking him if he wants to go into rehab. Here are the first two pages—the rest is private.

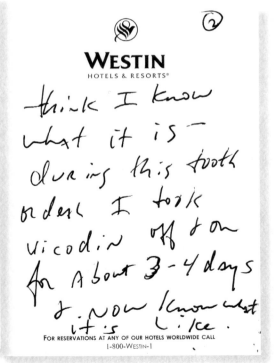

4:30 A.M. ①

WESTIN
HOTELS & RESORTS®

Hi baby,
I'm realizing
lately ~~that~~ (when
I can't sleep)-
that something
is "off" and I

FOR RESERVATIONS AT ANY OF OUR HOTELS WORLDWIDE CALL
1-800-WESTIN-1

WESTIN
HOTELS & RESORTS®

②

think I know
what it is -
during this tooth
ordeal I took
vicodin off & on
for about 3-4 days
& now know what
it's like.

FOR RESERVATIONS AT ANY OF OUR HOTELS WORLDWIDE CALL
1-800-WESTIN-1

After he reads the note the next morning, he says, "I was hoping you'd suggest that—in fact, I was thinking the same thing myself. **And just so ya know? It was my idea first.**"

And he went. No real surprise there. Everything either of us suggested for the other that was helpful, **we did.** You could call it "showin' off for each other" . . . or, you could call it

"love."

Geo handles rehab the way he handles everything— with grace and style. Afterward, I write him this card.

Sal and Geo leaving a restaurant:
Sal: How'd ya like dinner?
Geo (after getting sober): I had fun and I didn't even drink.

A STAR TREATMENT STORY

Speaking of chocolate, one time we're in a restaurant—Il Forno, in Santa Monica. Everybody is staring at Geo because they're wondering why, at the end of the meal, he's taking twenty or thirty pills. Vitamins. I'm only taking one. "Methadone," I say to the lady at the next table who can't take her eyes off of him. "Keeps me drug free, addicted to methadone. That way I don't get addicted to taking pills. It's a little secret of mine. Here, want one?" I ask. "Some people call them Altoids, but I don't."

Then the waiter comes by and asks us what we want for dessert. Geo says, **"Chocolate cake"** and I say, *"Chocolate cake."* We both say,

chocolate cake.

The waiter says, "All right. I'll bring **chocolate cake.**" Then Geo goes to the bathroom, and the waiter

AS TIME HAS GONE BY...

Dear Geo,

"One day at a time" with you is one more day in paradise —

...Some things change, but not my love for you. which is all right by me.

Love always + more,
Sal

returns with cake. But it's not **chocolate cake**—they don't have any **CHOCOLATE CAKE**—it's a white sponge cake with chocolate mousse on top. And the waiter says, "I don't think George Carlin is gonna want this because it's not really **chocolate cake."**

I say, "Well, leave it anyhow."

He says, "Ah, it's not real *chocolate cake,* so I don't think George Carlin is gonna want to eat it."

I say, "Well, leave it anyhow."

And he says, "But I don't think George Carlin is gonna want it—do you?"

So I stick my finger in it then lick it—and say, "Even if he doesn't, it's too late now, dude . . . Also, would you mind bringing a little extra whipped cream? Because this chocolate mousse tastes like shit. And I don't think George Carlin's gonna want it because it tastes nothing like chocolate cake."

Then Geo comes back from the bathroom and says, "There's been a finger in my food!"

I said, "Yeah, but I got rid of it."

And he said, "That's because you're my woman; always **protecting and looking out for me.**"

I said, "That's what I'm here for! I never pass up the opportunity to serve and protect my man, and I never will."

The other patrons in the restaurant who are staring at us applaud. Like I said, we both show off when we're together—*a lot.* But I had to work a little harder, exaggerate my movements so they'd know I was in the room.

Sweet Baby-Baby!

The truffles wish—they only wish—they were as sweet as you. But they'll never make it. You are all the sugar there ever was—and all the honey there will ever be. You make aspartame taste like SALT. You are maple syrup, molasses and fructose combined, times 10 million. I miss the sweet taste of your mouth, cookies. I'll be home soon to give you a squeeze. STAY SWEET— GEO'GIE

CHAPTER 19

Crystals, Trolls, Fairies & Elves

TO MY LOVE—

TWO TREES—

GROWING TOGETHER.

YOU,

ME.

BLOSSOMING.

ROOTED.

ALIVE.

GEORGE

SARAH ← ♡(GEORGE)

You have

ENCHAANTIFIED

this relationship.

You have spiritual

poise, girl.

I am different now.

WHASSUP? **TRUMP MARINA** GODDAMN!
HOTEL · CASINO

1-800-777-8477

YOU HAVE A GOOD CONNECTION

A PERSON YOU LOVE — BIG G.

As Jupiterians, we believe in fairies, elves, crystals, and trolls.
In fact, we communicate with lots of nature spirits, including trees and ordinary rocks. We even develop a new appreciation for cement, so as not to be discriminatory.

We have his, mine, and "our" crystals. If I'm worrying about a performance of his, I lay my crystals out on a photograph of him, so they gather positive energy and release it. After the show is over, he often comes offstage to tell me that he's just had another breakthrough performance.

Jupiter Geo and Sal's stage crystals in Geo's capable hands

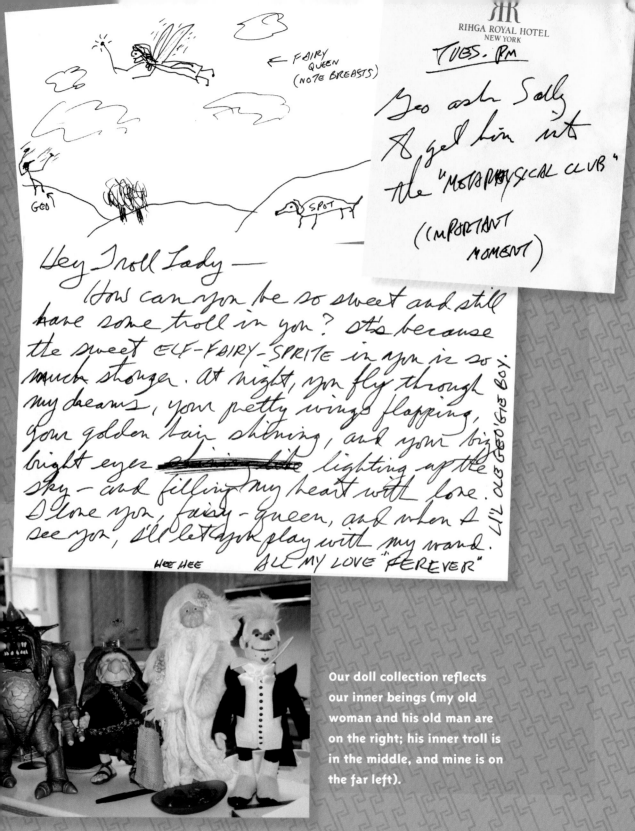

Our doll collection reflects our inner beings (my old woman and his old man are on the right; his inner troll is in the middle, and mine is on the far left).

I once explain to Geo that the Devic Kingdom is the realm where the power of the elements resides, and that it bestows on us the magic and good fortune provided by the fairies, elves, and trolls.

4

GEOGIE SAID (AND SO DID GEORGE) "GIMME A PASSPORT TO THAT DEVIC (PRON. DAY-VIK) KINGDOM. IN FACT, I WANT A RESIDENT VISA." HE HOPED IT WAS A TAX FREE ZONE.

HE ALSO SAID, "YA KNOW, SAL, YOU'VE BROUGHT SOME GREAT THINGS INTO MY LIFE, AND I'M VERY, VERY THANKFUL. I LOVE YOU IN A WAY THE POETS WOULD NEVER EVEN ATTEMPT TO DESCRIBE."

"WE ARE BEING IMAGINED."

— SALLY

"WE HAVE ENTERED A PLACE WHERE IMAGINATION IS IMAGINING ITSELF."

BALLY'S
LAS VEGAS
25th Anniversary

SAL —

DO IT FOR THE FAIRIES!

GEO

IT'S NOT OUR IMAGINATION, IT'S IMAGINATION IMAGINING US."

We call ourselves the "Clever Clown" and the "Sacred Fool." This note is posted on our refrigerator door:

The Sacred Fool of the tarot deck and the Clever Clown of trickster myth remind us that there is "nonsense in dogma and sense in nonsense; that opposites are each contained in the other, light in darkness, growth in decay, good in bad, and vice versa."

LOVE TO SALLY, TOO — MY SWEET GIFT from HEAVEN

SIGNED MR. 1937

SAL BABY —

Am really gonna miss you — the way I always do. Because everything I need in this world comes from you, my love. You are my be-all and end-all. When I'm away from you, I'm on loan from heaven — and I can't wait to be back where I belong. YOUR GEORGE

ME, SMILING.

* THE HEALTH-FOLD VARIETY

YOU ARE MY ETERNAL FLAME

GEO

DREAM

HEY FOREST GIRL !
I LOVE YOU SO
MUCH MY HEART WANTS
TO EXPLODE WITH JOY.
YOU'RE MY RAINBOW,
MY WOODS-GODDESS AND
THE ETERNAL STREAM
OF MY ~~XXXXXX~~ SOUL.
          YOUR CO-TROLL

FIND A
"MOON BOX."
for ME + SAL

HERE'S A FULL
MOON KISS for
          YOU

I LOVE YOU
SAL BABY.

Dreamstreet 1.
        ...e Smith 1987

SAL + GEO PARKED
AND WALKED INTO
THE WOODS.
THE TROLLS TAUGHT
THEM TO DREAM—
AND THEY DID.
      — STORY MAN

P.O. Box 9054, 3506 GB Utrecht, The Netherlands

CATCH

MILWAUKEE WI 552
PM
JAN
2003

3C USA

26

OZARK SAL

F
AL

IF.
60

PC 1807

DEAR SALLY,

TWO HEARTS

FOREVER.

EACH DAY YOU'RE
DOING THE THINGS
THAT ARE NEEDED
FOR THAT DAY.
ALL OTHER THINGS
ARE FOR TOMORROW.

— WISE OLD MAN

I LOVE YOU.

YOUR GEORGE

I've always believed there was more in this lifetime. Geo also believed there was more. But like everybody else—except Spot, of course—we don't know what that is.

Wise Old Man

Spot creates his own church, called

"THE CHURCH OF FALSE PROPHECY,"

dedicated to the belief that because everyone thinks they know the answer, no one really does, because every answer is different. Therefore, his is the only religion that purports to tell the truth.

GEO SEZ: God sez, "These people! Jesus! What did I get into? Next time I make a planet with just plants!"

I'm a plant!

When I met you,
they ran out of ways
to fuck with me

I'm SWIMMIN' in
the soup of
YOUR LOVE!

One day I say to Geo, "I have respect for all belief systems, but concerning atheism, how can you not believe in something that doesn't exist? Isn't that a double negative?" After that, I notice he doesn't mention that he's an atheist anymore. Instead, in public, he refers to himself as a "lapsed agnostic." He may have done if before then, but there was a special emphasis afterward with an annoying glance at Sal.

He leaves himself open to all other options. And I've seen him **pray.**

At night. Kneeling beside the bed. Out loud. But while a George Carlin prayer is sincere, it's unlike any other. There are few biblical references, and God knows him as "Mr. Wade" so word won't get out to his atheist followers. He says, "God, Mr. Wade here. You probably haven't been listening to me lately, and you really screwed up that one simple thing I asked ya to do yesterday. But here we are again, and I'm ready to give you another chance. That's what a great guy I am."

SARA
YOU'RE THE ONLY ANGEL THERE IS. AND YOU'RE MY ANGEL, SO I'M A LUCKY SOUL.

LUV

THE LITTLE ELECTRON

GOD IS ASTONISHED AS THE TWO SHOW UP AT CHURCH. ON WALL ST, NO LESS!

COUPLES 1st TRINITY JOKE

IT WAS TRINITY CHURCH — SO NAMED FOR GEO., SAL + SPOT.

Our first trinity joke

Magic.

LIVE HARD

JUPITER — THAT'S THE REAL NAME FOR HEAVEN.

SILVER—

You're the most living fuckin',
creature that a ~~[crossed out]~~ (really greative
god, who cared about LOVE,
(..[TENDER HEARTS]..)
~~[crossed out]~~ ~~[crossed out]~~,

SWEET BEAUTY AND ~~#~~ FIERCE
INDIVIDUALITY ~~([crossed out])~~

WOULD ~~NEVER~~ CONSIDER
^
PLACING INSIDE SUCH
A ~~[crossed out]~~ BEAUTIFUL,
GRACEFUL AND, SUCCULENT
BODY AS YOURS.

I AM YOURS, PERMANENT!

GEORGE

"Yours, Permanent!"

WHEN HEALTH ISSUES ABRUPTLY TAKE A TURN FOR THE WORSE FOR SPOT, we try every treatment available for dogs with cancer, including experimental stem cell research, by dragging him around the country, and nothing helps. He was put to sleep by our vet at home, at the age of seventeen, and although he abruptly makes his transition to the other side, he continues to speak through me. In fact, he immediately popped into "His Ghostly Presence," usually wanting a specific food or alcoholic beverage. Geo and I are both shocked, but maybe the shocking thing is that *here* and *there* are really the same place . . . our dining room. It's hard to ignore the fact that he's still around, especially when the wine cellar is empty. Geo and I both notice him. Maybe it was a prelude for me also being in touch with Geo now, but that doesn't negate the fact that Spot still has a presence (and a voice) all his own.

Arm itches, from
writing probably

"The Crystal Café"

Geo's writing to Sal takes a spiritual slant. In a story he writes to cheer her up about Spot passing over to the other side, he also uses it as an opportunity for another marriage proposal.

MAN AND WOMAN, LONER, COUNTERMAN   "THE CRYSTAL CAFÉ"

WOMAN: WE JUST BLEW IN FROM BAY CITY. THIS GUY WANTS ME TO MARRY HIM AND MOVE TO BELIZE AND BALI.

LONER: I WOULDN'T GO TO EITHER PLACE WITHOUT PLENTY OF CRYSTALS. NOT JUST THE CLEAR KIND, ~~PLENTY~~ PLENTY OF PINK ONES, TOO.

COUNTERMAN: I HAD A LADY ONCE GAVE ME A PINK CRYSTAL. ALSO GAVE ME A CLEAR ONE. ~~~~ SHE WAS SO PRETTY, THAT LADY — SALLY. I'LL NEVER FORGET HER. I CAN STILL FEEL THE TOUCH OF HER HAND. SHE TOOK MY SOUL SPECIAL PLACES, AND THEN SHE BROUGHT IT BACK AND TREATED IT WITH KINDNESS AND LOVE AND GREAT TENDERNESS. WE MADE THE MADDEST KIND OF PHYSICAL LOVE AND TOOK GREAT JOY IN EACH OTHERS'. I MISS HER.

MAN: WHAT HAPPENED TO HER?

COUNTERMAN: SHE WENT TO JUPITER.

WOMAN: GET OUT.

COUNTERMAN: NO KIDDING!

LONER: WHY'D SHE GO?

COUNTERMAN: HER DOG GOT SICK. SPOT. HE'S GOT A DISEASE THEY CAN ONLY CURE ON JUPITER. BECAUSE OF THE METHANE AND THE GRAVITY. SHE'LL BE BACK HERE IN TWO WEEKS, THE DOG'S ALL BETTER NOW. WHEN SALLY GETS BACK, WE'RE GOING TO GET MARRIED. THEN WE'RE GOING TO EXPAND THIS JUICE & BAGEL JOINT AND OPEN A NEW STORE ON THE SPANISH GOLD COAST AND MAKE LOVE AND BURRITOS FOREVER. FROM A MAN WITH HIS GLAND IN HIS HAND

I ♥ LOVE SALLY + SALLY LOVES ME ♥ = HEAVEN

I will always be at your side.

THE PINK CRYSTAL IS DOING JUST FINE.

GOODNIGHT, PRECIOUS GIFT.

Sally:
You're a prayer answered.

— the guy

Love,
your guy

WEST 54TH STREET, NEW YORK, NEW YORK 10019
(212) 307-5000

We get two more cockers named Goofy and Gertie. Goofy was born on Geo's birthday, Gertie's birthday is a few days after Sal's. They don't talk like Spot does. It was a huge transition when they moved in, but Spot didn't want to leave the house unguarded. Neither one of them takes the place of Spot (and he knows and approves of that; in fact, we believe Spot chose them because he left a quarter on our car seat the day we met them).

Gertie & Geo smooching

Goofy, as a puppy

CHAPTER 19½

Gertie & Goofy

Susan Jordan © 1994

Gertrude Elizabeth Carlin Wade

(aka Gertie) enjoys bossing Goofy around, has a neighborhood squirrel as a BFF, and she loves to smooch.

She also had a seizure one day, but she snapped out of it to chase a cat.

Buster Hudson Wade Carlin

(aka Goofy), although officially blind, is fine as long as you bring him water and cookies on the bed. (And don't mind if he farts in your face.)

A card from Geo about Goofy. As you can see from this picture, Geo had a favorite hat with "Live Hard" written across the bill, until the cleaners ruin it. At the time, I wanted to do a show called Talking to My Self, *and his current show was* I Kinda Like it When a Lot of People Die.

(WHO WAS INTERESTED IN MAGIC CARPETS AND SOLD THEM ON THE SIDE)

MATERIAL. SAL DID A SHOW CALLED "I KINDA LIKE IT WHEN A LOTTA PEOPLE FLY." AND, BECAUSE SAL WAS A SLENDER, GRACEFUL WOMAN, I DID A SHOW CALLED "TALKIN' TO MY SYLPH." WE WERE A BIG SUCCESS.

ALSO, OUR DOG, ALI BEN GOOFS, WON NUMEROUS AWARDS AT THE PERSIAN KENNEL CLUB'S ANNUAL SHOW IN "MEDICINE-SQUARE HANGING GARDENS." HIS BEST CATEGORY: MOST STUBBORN IN THE KINGDOM.

AND WE ALL LIVED HAPPILY EVER AFTER.

LOVE from
MR. TALL-TAILS,
GEO THE FUNNY

EGG WHITE GOONK →

HEY GOILY-GOIL! ← START HERE!

THIS IS AN ACTUAL PHOTOGRAPH OF ME IN A PAST LIFE, WRITING A CARD TO MY SWEETHEART, THE PERSIAN BEAUTY, HER HIGHNESS, PRINCESS ELI-BAN-SARA JANE, RULER OF ALL ANCIENT PERSIA — PLUS BUCKCREEK, A LITTLE KNOW OASIS ON THE DESERT. BUCKCREEK WAS KNOW FOR IT'S SATURDAY NIGHT WHORE HOUSE.

ANYWHO — I WAS QUITE THE GUY IN THOSE DAYS. THE BASEBALL CAP HADN'T COME INTO VOGUE YET, SO I AFFECTED A LOVELY CUSTOM-WRAPPED TURBAN WITH AN ANCIENT PIECE OF WISDOM LETTERED ON THE SIDE.

FOOD STAINS)

SARA AND I GOT MARRIED AND RULED ALL OF THE ANCIENT WORLD — INCLUDING HERMOSA BEACH, WHERE WE TOOK TURNS DOING EACH OTHER'S

JUST ANOTHER DAY AT 441.

XXXX

I LOVE YOU, SWEET SALLY. AND I WILL MISS YOU EVERY MINUTE I AM AWAY. BUT I'M NOT AWAY—I'M IN YOUR HEART, AND NEXT TO YOU IN BED. AND YOU'VE NEVER LEFT MY HEART IN 5 YEARS. ♡ ♡ ♡ ♡

SALLY—SWEETLOVE:

THE FAIRIES ARE KEEPIN' AN EYE ON US + KEEPIN' US SAFE.

THE TROLLS ARE MAKIN' SURE EVERYONE PAYS THEIR TROLL WHEN GOIN' OVER THOSE DELL CANAL BRIDGES. BUT GOOFY AND GERTIE HAVE BEEN SWIMMIN' ACROSS, AVOIDIN' THE TROLLS, NOT PAYIN', AND THE CHIEF TROLL IS GETTIN' PISSED. HIS NAME IS BUSHTROLL AND HE'S GONNA SEND RUMSTROLL TO BOMB OUR YARD. GOOFY TOLD HIM THAT OUR YARD HAD ALREADY BEEN BOMBED BY HIM + GERTIE AND THEY HAD USED CHEMICAL WEAPONS, TOO, IN THEIR INFAMOUS

GIRLY—

LOOK AT LI'L SARA JANE— TRYIN' TO GET 6 (HOURS MORE) OF SLEEP. BUT GEORGIE SAID SOMETHIN' FUNNY —AN' SARRY COULDN'T HELP HERSELF. SHE STARTED LAUGHIN' & LAUGHIN'— SO HARD THAT SHE WOKE UP GOOFY IN THE YARD. SO GERTIE BIT GOOFY'S EAR AND GOOFY BEAT THE SHIT OUT OF GERTIE. THEN THEY MADE UP AND TOOK A DOUBLE DUMP —RIGHT ON THE SIDEWALK. GERTIE THOUGHT IT WAS FUNNY, SO SHE THREW UP ON HER BED AND THEN CIRCLED THE YARD 700 TIMES AT A FAST PACE, WITHOUT STOPPIN'.

A double dump

Bushtroll and Rumstroll

I LOVE YOU MADLY. I MISS YOU BADLY.

"PEE-PEE/POO-POO" BOMBING MISSIONS— LED BY THE INTREPID COLONEL SARA JANE WADE, SPECIAL FORCES COMMANDER. ~~THEY~~ BUSHTROLL IMMEDIATELY SURRENDERED AND GAVE G+G A COUPLA COOKIES AS A GESTURE OF GOODWILL. G+G TESTED THE COOKIES WITH THEIR CHEMICAL FIELD-TESTING KITS. THEY WERE FOUND TO CONTAIN BEEF AND TURKEY, SO THEY REFUSED TO EAT THEM AND BIT BUSHTROLL ON THE BALLS.

— FINIS

LOVE, THE WAR CORRESPONDENT

To Goofy & Gertie—the G-Twins

TO THE G-TWINS!

Hi KIDS. I RAN INTO THIS LITTLE GUY IN VIRGINIA (ASK YER MOM TO SHOW YA VIRGINIA ON THE MAP). HE WANTED YOU TO SEE THE LATEST THING WHEN IT COMES TO TAKIN' OVER YOUR DOG-PARENTS' BED-ROOM. IN FACT, HE SAYS, HE'S GONE SO FAR AS TO ASK HIS DOG-FOLKS TO START SLEEPIN' IN ANOTHER ROOM – SAYS HE NEEDS THE EXTRA SPACE TO SPREAD OUT. HE BOUGHT THE FAN AT A FLEA MARKET WHERE HE WENT TO SELL HIS EXTRA FLEAS – SAYS HE GETS A NICKLE APIECE FROM A GROOMER WHO PUTS 'EM ON POODLES AS A WAY OF GETTIN' EVEN WITH THE FRENCH. TAKES ALL KINDS.

I'LL BE HOME + SEE YA ON MONDAY, SO SHAPE UP + GET SHARP. I'M HOPIN' YER MOM IS GONNA GIVE ME A GOOD REPORT ON YOU TWO DELINQUENTS — OTHERWISE, YOU LOSE YOUR TELEVISION PRIV-ELIGES; NO MORE ANIMAL PLANET AND SCOOBY DOO + LASSIE – AND NO MORE POOCH PORN ON THE COMPUTERS. THAT STUFF IS DISGUSTING ANYWAY — GREAT DANES HUMPIN' CHIHUAHAS!!! GOD! SAY HELLO TO YER MA + TELL HER I LOVE HER.

One more Mother's Day card

MOM —

DAD STOLE MY CARD
TO YOU BEFORE I
SENT IT, SO YOU COULD
HAVE A CARD TO SEND
TO YORE MOM.
I HOPE SHE'S HAPPY NOW!
    SIGNED,
    "INDIGNANT ON THE CHAIR"
LOVE, GERTIE

Happy Mother's Day
    from
your little nonconformist.

LOVE (GERTIE)

    I'M GLAD ~~DAD~~ YOU
DIDNY STEEL THIS CARD TO
GIVE TO DAD TO SEND TO HIS
MOM. I UNDERSTAND SHE
DIED IN 1985. TOO BAD.
BUT AT LEAST YOU GOT THIS
            CARD.

*These ladies remind Geo of my mother
and her best friend, Martha East*

CHAPTER 20

Mom & Geo

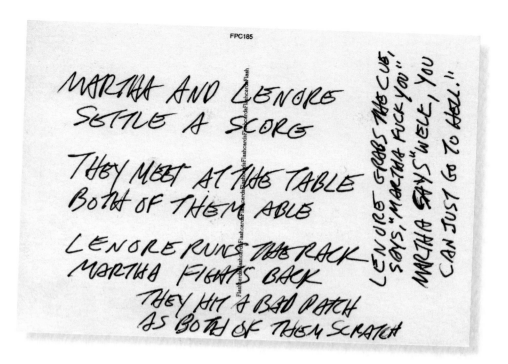

FPC185

MARTHA AND LENORE
SETTLE A SCORE

THEY MEET AT THE TABLE
BOTH OF THEM ABLE

LENORE RUNS THE RACK
MARTHA FIGHTS BACK
THEY HIT A BAD PATCH
AS BOTH OF THEM SCRATCH

LENORE GRABS THE CUE
SAYS, "MARTHA FUCK YOU"
MARTHA SAYS "WELL, YOU
CAN JUST GO TO HELL."

Concerning my mother who's never tasted alcohol:

SAL: How do you know if you're an alcoholic if you've never tasted alcohol?

GEO: If you can't stop drinkin' water!

My mom and Geo are so much alike I felt as if I'd married my mother. In fact, it's hard to tell them apart. The only difference is, my mother's never tasted alcohol. Plus, she's the daughter of a Baptist minister from Ipswich, South Dakota, and she doesn't curse. Other than that, they're just alike. If she's really mad, she'll say, "Oh, crap!"—but you had to have really crossed the line; like, smoked crack or something.

And she doesn't mind if I talk about her in public (in case you were wondering)—as long as I don't tell people she's my mother. "George Carlin's mother-in-law from the Ozarks" is all right—Mom says she doesn't mind being called that.

WHAT MOM WEARS WHEN SHE COMES TO VISIT FROM THE OZARKS . . .

So as not to insult her, I tell her to bring at least one outfit that she considers "church wear." But instead, she wears pants she bought at Kmart, called "bend-over pants" with an elastic front panel, so you can eat all you want and still sit down. They'll expand to accommodate any size meal. Handy for traveling, Spot thinks.

"Isn't that called maternity apparel?" Spot asks.

And she wears a pair of nurse's shoes that she tries to pass off as Reebok athletic wear because they're white. "Sorry, Reeboks," Geo says. She also has a collection of sweatshirts that have outdoor scenes made of glitter and sequins that she glued on herself—for example, on one is a bear in a tree, and the bear has a fish in its mouth with a hook in it. And the hook is real. So is the fish. "The lake is fake! For that, you can tell she just splashed herself with water," I say to Geo, knowing she can fool him, but not me since we're both related.

Not to be outdone by her sequins and glitter, Geo goes out and buys a box of fairy stickers to add to his notes to me.

ARE YOU POOKY-DOODLE OR PEEKY-DOODLE? I FORGOT.

LUV

BAD ART

GEO

SAL

RIHGA ROYAL HOTEL
NEW YORK

AT NYE

ash SALLY re:

HER KINDERGARTEN STORY

TRUE FACT: My mother, the daughter of a Baptist minister, taught me all the books of the Bible by the time I was in kindergarten. (Because I showed an aptitude for language and an ear for odd-sounding words, even at that early age.) All thirty-nine books in the Old Testament, twenty-seven in the New—sixty-six in all. Then, she carted me around to all her friends' houses to show me off as I recited them, as if I were a parrot. "And afterwards," I tell Geo, "as a reward—"

"She gave you a cracker?" he answers.

"Right!" I say. "And, as an alternative to public school? She enrolled me in a rescue and adoption group for parrots, where instead of selling Girl Scout cookies, we went door to door—"

"Selling saltines?"

"You've heard this story before, huh?"

"Right," he says, "it was all over the news," then makes a note to show me he wants to hear more later.

In the beginning, my dear ol' mother's never even heard of George Carlin. The name means nothing to her. In fact, one day she calls me in Atlantic City—and, because I've told her I'm staying with George Carlin, she asks for him and they patch her through to the box office instead of our room, and then ask her how many tickets she wants. So she thinks I'm playin' Atlantic City, even though she's never heard of me either, apparently, or why else wouldn't she ask for my room?

Like I said, I can't tell Mom and Geo apart at times.

Neither of them "got" Elevator Etiquette.

On an elevator, suddenly, it seems, their IQs drop as fast as the elevator does. Geo talks about the other people beside him as if they're deaf. My mother does the same thing. In fact, when they're together, they talk to each other about the people beside us, which is doubly embarrassing. What they don't seem to realize is that although they lower the tone of their voices, the volume is still the same.

Mom: Look at those shoes . . . how can she walk in those?

Geo: Maybe she's from a circus and learned to walk on stilts.

Mom: Did they think they could wear white in the wintertime and get away with it?

Geo: Apparently so! And look at the honker in the middle of that kid's face. Wonder why they take him out in public . . .

Mom (*giggling*): Oh, George!

I pretend I don't know them and get off at a different floor.

> **Make me a bird so that I can fly far, far away.**

In Vegas, at the MGM, in the section of the hotel that's for performers, there's an elevator in the middle of the room, for those too lazy to carry their luggage up the stairs they've also provided. Well, my mother rides up and down the elevator as if she's at an amusement park, counts the telephones in the suite—twenty-three in all—then calls my brother and gives him a report. "There's one on each end of the bathroom!" she whispers.

"That's because if you're taking a dump, you might get an idea you want to tell somebody," Geo says to her when she tells him about it.

"Oh, George" she says again, and giggles.

Mom and Geo are both picky eaters. I take them to a five-star restaurant.

"Actually, it's a four-star restaurant; 'cause when you sit beside the window and look outside, you can only see four stars," I point out.

"On a clear day, five," Geo says.

"What's steak tartare?" my mother asks. "Is that the stuff that gets stuck on your teeth?"

Geo doesn't know what it is either. I can tell because he asks for his tartare medium rare. I order chicken, Mom orders duck—a cornish hen, actually, but she calls it a duck. And when the food comes, she sits there frowning at her food, as if she doesn't like what's on her plate. Her duck's half the size of my chicken—and I've got half a chicken, she's got a whole duck. So I explain, "Well, that's because **ducks** by nature are smaller than chickens. So even if I had one breast of a chicken, it's gonna be bigger than your whole duck—they didn't cheat you on purpose. It's nothing personal. And I certainly didn't bring you all this way from Buck Creek, Missouri, just to eat in front of you once you ran out of duck. That would've been rude."

"Oh, crap," she says disappointedly.

Geo suggests, helpfully, that she bait the fishhook on her sweatshirt with bread from the breadbasket, then lean over the nearby fish tank to see if she can't catch something bigger to eat. She thinks it's funny. The two of them laugh at that, while I busy myself with putting more of my food on her plate.

HERE'S SOMETHING ELSE MY MOTHER AND GEO AGREE ON . . . BOB DOLE NEVER SHOULD HAVE DONE THOSE ERECTILE DYSFUNCTION COMMERCIALS.

My mother said, "I don't think Bob Dole should've ever done those ED commercials. Because he ran for president. I think you should do one or the other—but not both."

"You mean the ones where really he's talkin' 'bout assholes *and* crotches on TV?" Geo comments. "Neither do I."

Also, my mom and Geo both call President George Bush "George," because they don't think he really won the election. That's two presidents my mother and George Carlin agree on. How many more do you need?

**They also wait until the top of the eleven o'clock news—
and *then* decide to tell personal stories.** Just when I'm about to hear
the most important news of the day, they start going on and on, seemingly about every little thing
that's ever happened to them since the day they were born. George even talks about *being* born
and how his mother almost aborted him.

Then he chooses to share about how he got kicked out of middle school and went to
boarding school, and then he got kicked out of boarding school and went back to middle
school, and the nuns said, "Let's take a vote," and everybody voted him back in as long as
he'd write the school play, which saved the day.

AS THEY FIRST ENTERED BATTERY
PARK, GEO SAW AN
OLD BUILDING IN THE DIS-
TANCE WHICH HE THOUGHT
WAS THE ORIGINAL BLDG.
THAT HOUSED THE GUNS OF
THE BATTERY. AS THE COUPLE
DREW CLOSER, THOUGH, HE
RECOGNIZED HIS GRAND-
MOTHER — LOOKING FOR
CHANGE ON THE GROUND.
"IT HAS TO BE HER," HE
SAID "THIS IS WHERE
SHE SNEAKED INTO AMER-
ICA ENABLING ME TO BE
NEARLY ABORTED A FEW
MILES NORTH."

More of Geo's personal history, from a Jupiterian story, written at Battery Park in New York

My mother's story, meanwhile, is what we call the "Mindy and the Monkey" story.
Read it yourself and you'll find out why. By the time they've finished exchanging this
attention-grabbing information, poor Sal missed the top of the news.

MINDY & THE MONKEY

George Carlin's favorite story of mine, as told to me by my mother. In fact, he had me tell this to him so often, I have it memorized.

Mindy was married a year ago to Dan. And she was runnin' around with Dave. And Dave is the same age as her son Bob, who's nineteen. Then Mindy told my mother that she and Dave were goin' to move to Myrtle Beach. Then last fall Mindy told my mother she was datin' a guy named Jim. But still livin' with Dave's mother. Then she called in December and told my mother that in February she was going to marry Jim.

Then, six weeks ago, my mother went to the lake, and Mindy was married to Frank. He was Jim's friend. And she's still livin' with Dave's mother. And she calls her "Mom." But Dave doesn't live there anymore. He's wound up back in Kansas City 'cause he's only nineteen.

And when Mindy got divorced? Dan got the monkey. The monkey's name is Amy. And here's the good news: When she married Frank, Mindy got the monkey back 'cause last weekend Dan, the one Mindy was married to, wanted to stay at the lake with them 'cause it was cheaper than rentin' his own place. And he thought they had a spare room, but when he got there, they gave it to Amy—the monkey—and put him out on the porch. So he got mad and left.

So . . . that's how Mindy got the monkey back.

"And here we all are out here in California," I add, "livin' mundane lives, monkey-free."

"Except for Paris Hilton," Spot says.

(By the way, I'm mimicking my mother because I read somewhere that if you mimic the person you're around, they'll like you better. In fact, I think I read it in the Bible.)

COOKS—

I DON'T CARE HOW
BAD IT MAKES YOU FEEL—
HAPPY FUCKIN'
            BIRTHDAY.

NEXT STEP—SOCIAL
            SECURITY.

THEN YOU & MOM CAN SWAP
STORIES ABOUT HOW LATE
THE CHECKS ALWAYS ARE.

ONE MORE THING MY MOM &
GEO AGREE ON . . .

LADY—
    YOU'VE ACTUALLY HAD
    ONLY ONE BIRTHDAY.

    ONE WAS ALL YOU NEEDED.*

        YOUR LOVE BUG

* AND FRANKLY, ONE WAS ALL THE REST OF US COULD HANDLE.

INDIANA, 1955
PHOTOGRAPH BY ELLIOTT ERWITT

TO THE PERSON I WOULD DIE FOR—

EARLY PHOTOS SURFACE OF
GEORGE'S OLD ACT. IT WAS
BASED ON THE ECSTACY HE
FELT UPON RECEIVING PSYCHIC
REVELATIONS THAT SOMEDAY IN
THE FUTURE HE WOULD FALL IN
LOVE WITH SALLY WADE. THE
NEWS ECSTAFIES HIM, AND HE
DONS A LAMPSHADE (A TASTEFUL
LAMPSHADE IT SHOULD BE MEN-
TIONED) TO CELEBRATE HIS GREAT
GOOD LUCK. INCREDULOUS
TOWNFOLK GATHER TO MARVEL
AND MOCK HIS
PERFORMANCE.
THEY ALL DIE LATER AND ARE NEVER MISSED.

TO THE
SWEETEST,
LOVLIEST,
SEXIEST,
TALLEST WOMAN
I HAVE EVER HAD
THE PLEASURE
OF TONGUE-KISSING.
MY MISSY SALLY
from
CUTE CROTCH

2¢

CHAPTER 21

Mr. Stage Stud
The Performing Chapter

Gonna make some "green."

The secret to Geo's success (aside from being smarter and funnier than most) is that he always uses the color *green,* whenever he starts a new project, he tells me. In fact, he says to me one day, "You know why we're using green on this project?" "No, why?" "Because we're gonna make some money on it. I always choose a green folder and a green paper clip when I'm starting a new project, 'cause green means *money.* Gonna make some 'green.' In other words, this is gonna be a huge success. You make the project '*green*' and then you *make* some green."

"I see. So it's not for environmental purposes that we've 'gone green,'" I say. "It's that GREEN is the color of *money . . .* "

"Right."

Sal's first performance tip to Geo, which he saves and dates

GEO'S GROUNDBREAKING MEMORIZATION TECHNIQUE, AS TOLD TO SAL

"You recite the paragraph out loud, without looking at it, then you look at it and see if you got all the words right. If you missed a word, you circle it in red, and *repeat only the sentence that has that word in it, fifteen to twenty times.* That's the key," he told me. "You don't repeat the sentences that you already got right, because you already know them, and you have to trust that. So to repeat the paragraph is a b.f.w.o.t.,* when you could just be learning the word you forgot."

*** B.F.W.O.T.** *An Ozarkian expression for "big fucking waste of time."*

Not a bad observation I'm thinking, *for a kid who was kicked out of middle school, never went to college, and was told by his Air Force superior:* "Carlin, you enter the room like a **madwoman scattering shit!**" Which is the real reason, he says, he decided to always be organized.

Another thing Geo does that adds to his success is, when writing, he does the easiest stuff first. He doesn't call it "writing," he calls it *"moving things along."* Which means, he takes ideas that are unformed and indistinct and only improves them a little. Then he's satisfied for the time being, until it nudges him again. For example, his routine about "hating kids" was originally about, well, hating kids. Over time, it evolved into a piece about parents not allowing their kids any free time, thereby turning them into yuppie designer babies and status symbols. And usually, after using the piece in one of his HBO specials, it would evolve even more. "But perfection is never obtained, and that is **part of the game,**" he says.

Also, with the goal of his next HBO show in mind, he times his pieces down to the last second. I think having a goal in mind is more important than how many seconds a section lasts, but he disagrees, and shouts, "Forty-six seconds!" proudly, when he nails it.

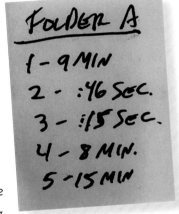

PACING BEHIND THE CURTAIN WITH GEO

On the road, I spent most of my time backstage, before the show, pacing behind the curtain as Geo rehearses his opening lines. When he turns, I turn. When he walks back the other way, I follow in his footsteps. As he repeats his opening lines, I recite whatever I'd say if I was going out there. We both like this ritual; it makes us feel connected and safe. The pacing takes up all my time though, so of course, I never have time to perform.

DID GEO TEACH SAL ABOUT COMEDY?

Geo tried to teach me about comedy, but I don't think yelling, "Faster, faster! **Louder, louder!** Say it with more confidence," teaches anybody anything about comedy. However, my persona played off of his, which gave me a certain degree of confidence that I otherwise never would've had. One of his biggest regrets, I believe, is that I already had my own style, so he couldn't come to my rescue like a knight in shiny armor. But that didn't stop him from trying.

And in spite of my stage fright, he relaxes me so much that one night I say to him, backstage in Vegas, "Hey! I could go over and actually kinda go on." He thinks this is such an important moment, he remembers it throughout his show and writes it down afterward.

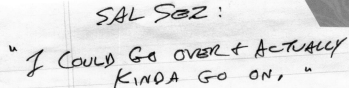

SAL SEZ:

" I COULD GO OVER + ACTUALLY KINDA GO ON. "

HELLO.

HEY CATERPILLAR —
C'MON OUT; THE STAGE IS FINE. PEOPLE ARE WAITIN' TO SEE YOU FLY.
ACTUALLY, YOU'VE BEEN A PRETTY BUTTERFLY ALL YOUR LIFE. I'M SURE GLAD YOU SETTLED ON MY FLOWER. I'M ALL THE BETTER FOR IT.
I'M SO IN LOVE WITH YOU. GEO'GIE

BUSTED SUSPENDERS

A card Geo writes for Sal after she wins a humor contest gossiping about Spot

Baker
Playtime

TO THE QUEEN,

THE BIG BABY HAS BEEN IN LAS VEGAS FOR SUCH A LONG TIME, THEY FINALLY PUT HIM IN THE BAND. CORDIALLY, YOUR SERVANT,
— STUDLEY STAGEMAN

MISS SALLY WADE

LAS VEGAS, NV 890
PM
26 OCT 1998

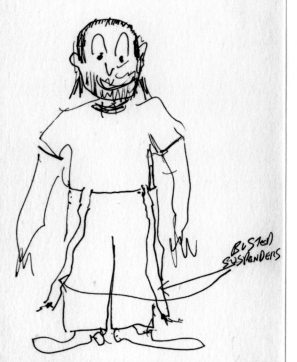

BUSTED SUSPENDERS

HEY COOKIE —
I KNOW YA AIN'T GONNA FOR-GOT ME — JUST A FLOWERY CARD FOR MY SWEET BLOSSOM. IT'S A LAZY SATURDAY IN FORT WAYNE, INDIANA. WATCHIN TV AND RE-PACKIN MY BAGS. THINKIN' HOW PROUD I AM OF YOU — DANCIN', EXERCISIN', GOIN' TO TOASTMASTERS AND TALKIN' ABOUT HOW GOOD IT FELT. WOW! WOT A GOIL! .. I'M SO PROUD. AND I'M SO HAPPY!!
I WISH I COULDA HEARD YER DAD-BLAMED SPEECH — I WOULDA BEEN BUSTIN' MY SUSPENDERS WITH PRIDE. LOVE GEO

GEO TAKES TIME OFF AND TAKES SAL OUT ON THE ROAD TO PERFORM.

We usually rent a car and drive around looking for clubs. Not that it isn't a fun trip, but all we do is drive and piss and bomb. We never stop for any other reason, except to search for spare change on the ground and in all the Coke machines. If we find a quarter, we flip it and ask the universe if we should go into a particular club or keep driving. If it's heads, we keep driving. If it's tails, I gotta go inside and perform. And if I bomb? Well, we call that

"Tantric Comedy."

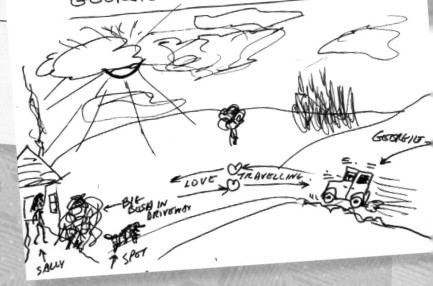

67 DAYS   FAX TO SALLY   TOGETH.-APART 48-19

LA 5 TOGETHER AT HOME 11/15-19
   3 APART 11/20-22
LA 2 TOGETHER AT HOME 11/23-24
   6 APART 11/25-11/30
LA 2 TOGETHER AT HOME 12/1-12/2
   1 APART 12/3
NYC 4 TOGETHER ON ROAD 12/4-12/7 N.Y.
   6 APART 12/8-12/13
LA 14 TOGETHER AT HOME 12/14-12/27
   7 FLA-TOGETHER AT KEY WEST 12/28-1/3
LA 10 TOGETHER 1/4-1/14
   3 APART 1/15-1/17
   3 TOGETHER/HOME 1/18-1/20
   - ROAD
   - THEN NYC PRE-HBO

NY 4
FLA 7
LA 37
ROAD 19
67 DAYS

TANTRIC COMEDY
GO 50 MIN BEFORE
ANYBODY LAUGHS &
(WITHOUT A GOAL
OF LAUGHTER
& THATS NOT
THE GOAL

"GEORGIE DRIVIN' HOME TO SALLY"

GEORGIE
LOVE ♡ TRAVELLING
BIG BUSH IN DRIVEWAY
SALLY
SPOT

SOMETIMES, EVEN GEORGE CARLIN CAN'T DRAG "CHICKEN LITTLE" ONSTAGE

Whenever we stop in a town and go to a club— big town, small club; small town, big club—either way, as soon as George Carlin walks in, it blows people's minds. It blows my mind! Everyone staring at him as if he's royalty. . . . Then Geo parades me up to the owner and asks him if I can perform. "Of course," he says. "Anything for you, George." But by then, I'm halfway out the door and more frightened than before.

GET OUTTA MY WAY! I'M COMIN' throuGH, BoyS.

And because of that, along with a delicious vanilla soy milk shake with non-fat chocolate cupcakes he has waiting - she agrees to go.
Love always,
Your Ms. everything.

sweet VoicE,
As All the neighborhood boys tease little Sarah Jane, telling her that she should have either "stayed home or worn a hat" Geogie continues to push her out on center stage where he knows she'll find fulfillment - because he'll ~~be waiting to push her home afterwards~~

Once I say to him, as I head out the door, "Well, I have no **dick jokes**."

He says, "Do you wanna ask the audience who they're gonna vote for—the Republiclits or the Democunts?"

"No! Let's get outta here."

"Okeydokey, **Artichokey!**"

GEO'S GUIDE TO NAME-CALLING FOR SAL

George Carlin gives other people permission to say the honest and unthinkable. But Geo gives Sal a list of words to use so that she won't have to curse onstage. Since guys use body parts when they call each other names (asshole, prick, dick, cunt, etc.), I ask him, "Have ya got anything female-specific?" This was the best he could do . . .

Sal's ready for her close-up

- **SCUMBAG**
- **JACKOFF**
- **FOOL**
- **KNAVE**
- **DOPEY**
- **STUPID**
- **BLASTED**
- **FREAKIN'**
- **FRIGGIN'**
- **DAMN**
- **DUMB**
- **FEEBLEMINDED**
- **DULL-WITTED**
- **MORONIC**
- **DUMBASS**
- **NOSE-HAIR PULLER**
- **NOSE-HAIR PICKER**
- **NOSE-HAIR PLUCKER**

PLEASE DO NOT RING OR KNOCK ON DOOR BEFORE 12:00 NOON.

THANKS, GEORGE C.

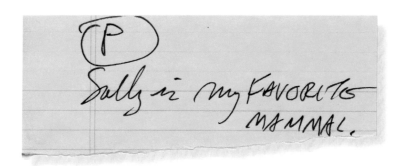

Sally is my FAVORITE MAMMAL.

A JOKE GEO GETS TIRED OF USING, THAT HE GIVES TO SAL

When Geo would first walk out onstage, he'd say, **"How y'all doin'?"** And after they applauded, he'd say, "Oh . . . yeah? Well, **fuck you!**" And when he got tired of using it, he gave it to me. I kept pestering him to use it again, but it was played out in his mind.

So one night I say to Geo, testing a line, "How do you know when you've been hanging out with George Carlin too long?"

"How?" he asks.

"Well, when my dear ol' mother from the Midwest called, I said, 'How y'all doin'?' And when she said, 'Oh, Jim's truck broke down on the freeway, and Mary Ann's pregnant for the third time, and my back went out beneath my bra strap where it itches sometimes, so I got an epidural . . .' I said, "Oh . . . yeah? Well, **fuck you!**" That's how you know when you've been hanging out with George Carlin too long."

When I tell Geo I improved on his joke by including my dear ol' mother, he says,

"That's what mothers are for! To help you become a better person!"

SAL IMITATING GEO:

Sal: Here's something Americans spend money on foolishly.

Geo: What?

Sal: Lowering the national debt.

WHEN IT'S NOT "SHOWTIME," IT'S "SHOW-OFF TIME"

After his show, we take turns, **hopping on the bed, ad-libbing material**.

Geo would talk about the government, and I'd talk about my mother. Sometimes we'd mix it up and I'd talk about the government and he'd talk about my mother. (Sorry, Mom!)

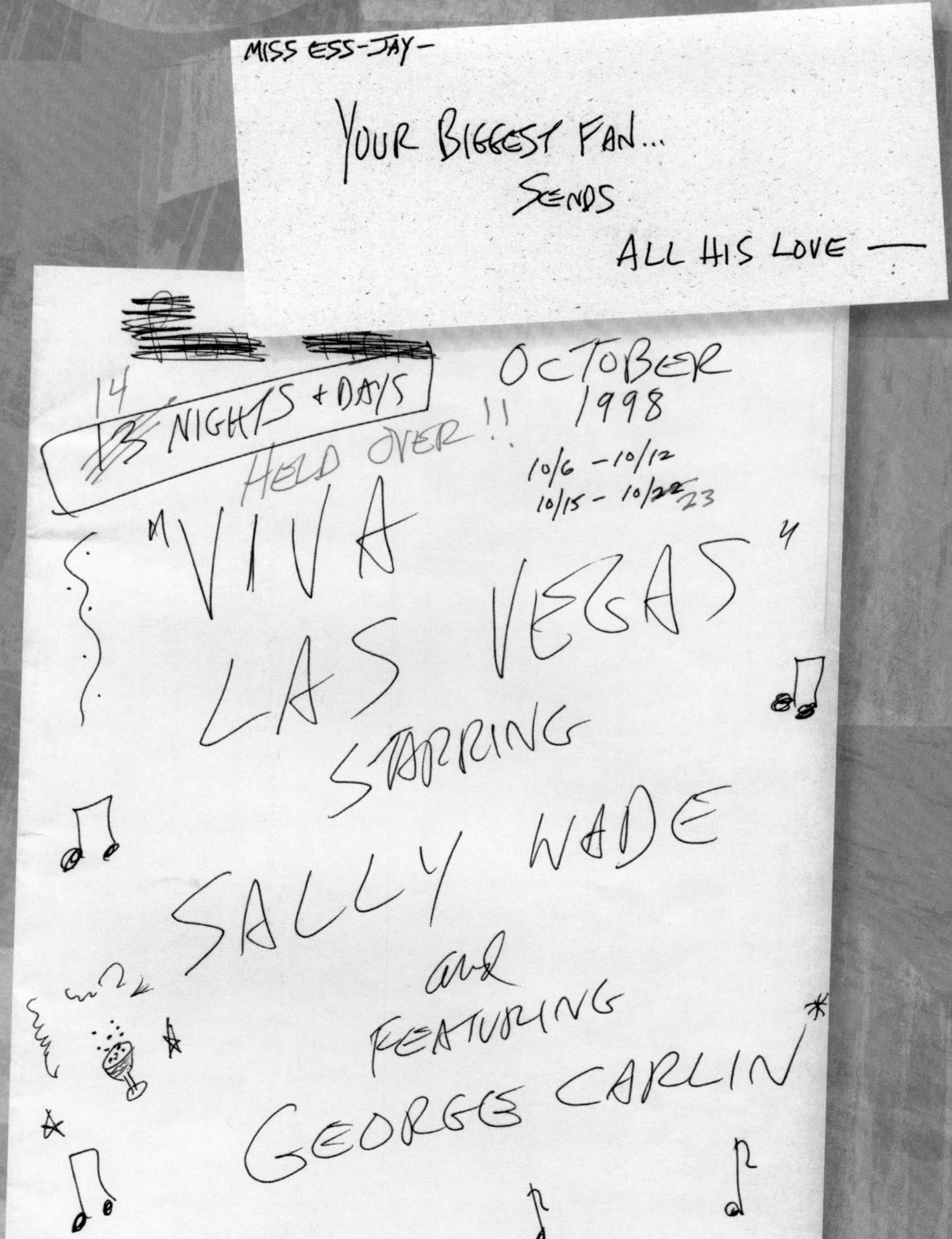
MISS ESS-JAY—
YOUR BIGGEST FAN...
SENDS
ALL HIS LOVE —
OCTOBER 1998
~~13~~ 14 NIGHTS + DAYS
HELD OVER!!
10/6 – 10/12
10/15 – 10/~~22~~ 23
"VIVA LAS VEGAS"
STARRING
SALLY WADE
and
FEATURING
GEORGE CARLIN*
* IN THE ROLE OF HIS LIFE

The Sunday Blat ✡✡✡

SAL SEZ, "MY SHOES HURT AND I'M TIPSY"

LAS VEGAS — APRIL 25 UPI

LAUGHING UPROARIOUSLY AND WALKING UNSTEADILY ON HER NEW JUPITER SHOES, QUEEN SAL MADE HER WAY DOWN THE BOULEVARD WITH HER SWEET CUPCAKE.…———

POST-CHINOIS SEX GREAT, COUPLE SAY

LAS VEGAS —— APRIL 25. AP

FOLLOWING A GREAT MEAL, WHICH INCLUDED FREE DESSERT THE HAPPY⟶

~~⟶⟶⟶⟶⟶⟶⟶⟶⟶~~

Hey Cookie —

Sometimes a guy can get lonely — sittin' on a piling, waitin' to do the last show —— only one ~~guy~~ PERSON in the aud-ience. Fortunately, after the sun goes down, he goes home to his sweet dreamy mama, the COOKIE of his HEART — the ~~biscuit~~ biscuit of his SOUL. She looks at him with loving eyes — and he eases into Paradise. Yours till the wata is gone.   YOUR LOVER MAN
                                    BIG GEO

Queen Kong &
Big Geo . . .

In reality, Sal is so afraid of performing that Geo calls her "Chicken Little, the ninety second comic. . . . Don't miss her! Get here early!" But in her mind, she's Sally Shitkicker, unplugged and uncensored, like Queen Kong.

You're the Queen Kong of my heart.

You can climb my skyscraper any time.

Big Geo

Geo's note quotes Sally Shitkicker

SALLY SHITKICKER SAYS!
RIHGA ROYAL HOTEL
NEW YORK

I don't do anything I don't want to do but I do a lot of things other people don't want me to do.

your material is strong.
When you take chances
with your (STRONG)
material — that's when
you get strong. Then
you can do no wrong.
STRONG YOU
STRONG MATERIAL —

Geo writes Sal notes of
encouragment.
He writes the word "strong"
five times in this note. Sal thinks
he's trying to convince her to
sound like him instead of
like Jack Benny.

YOU'RE DOIN'
SO WELL —

KEEP FEEDIN' THAT,

NOT THE CRITICAL
PERFECTIONIST
ASSHOLE
NAZI
PARENT!!

TO FEAR LADY

I HOPE YA VOMIT
EVERY NIGHT,
AND SHIT IN
YER PANTS ON STAGE.
AND KNOCK OVER YOUR TEA.

FROM
FEARLESS
FUCKO

HEY, SALLY!

FUCK
FEAR —

GOT THAT?
FUCK IT !
BLOW IT OFF!

When did Geo have time to write all these masterpieces, if he was out getting a bagel or picking up Frédéric Fekkai shampoo for Sal? (Frédéric Fuck-I, he calls it.)

Well, Spot claims, when Geo wasn't making him earn his keep in other ways (with street hustles, mainly—or ripping retired people off with insurance scams), he was up all night writing and hitting the gin. If he wrote a really good piece or faxed Geo a joke or an extra routine, Geo would even double the pain meds Spot took for hip dysplasia.

An avid reader of his reviews

In fact, Spot claims Geo changed several of his lines. You know that line Geo did where he shortened the list of Ten Commandments down to three? And the third one was *"Thou shalt be faithful to the provider of thy nookie"*? Spot says that should've been **"Thou shalt be faithful to the provider of thy cookie."**

And about that routine called **"Stuff"?** Well, Spot says that it was originally about dog bowls, chew toys, bones, ear medicine, and tennis balls. But since Geo doubled his pain meds, he didn't complain. "Wasn't the first time I've sold myself down the river," he says. "And probably won't be the last."

Hi Love —

I hope you ride this pretty horse right to Broadway — and beyond. He world needs to hear your wit and charm and sweet human-ness. I know how wonderful you are — I want the rest of to know. Stay at it, Sara June. I'll be right there with ya — MR STAGE STUD

ESS JAY

CHAPTER 22

Poetry & Artwork

Not everybody gets to come to this Earth and make imprints others will follow. But what most people don't know is that Geo made romantic imprints. **He's the** sweetest, *most loving*, **most giving,** liberated **man I've ever known.** I think his poetry and artwork reveal this best.

①

A COOKIE ON THE SAUCER;
A FAIRY IN THE CUP.
MY LOVE FOR SALLY WADE
GOES UP, UP, UP.

②

THE SAUCER 'NEATH THE COOKIE;
THE CUP ~~BENEATH~~ 'NEATH THE GIRL;

THE JOURNEY SALLY TAKES ME ON,
— PUTS ME IN A WHIRL.

THE GREAT POET

HULA SAL

THE SUN?   AN EGG?   ← HAT?

MISTAKENLY DRAWN LINES

Self-portrait by Sal

FLOYDEN

PLERF

DWENDER

KROOM

264

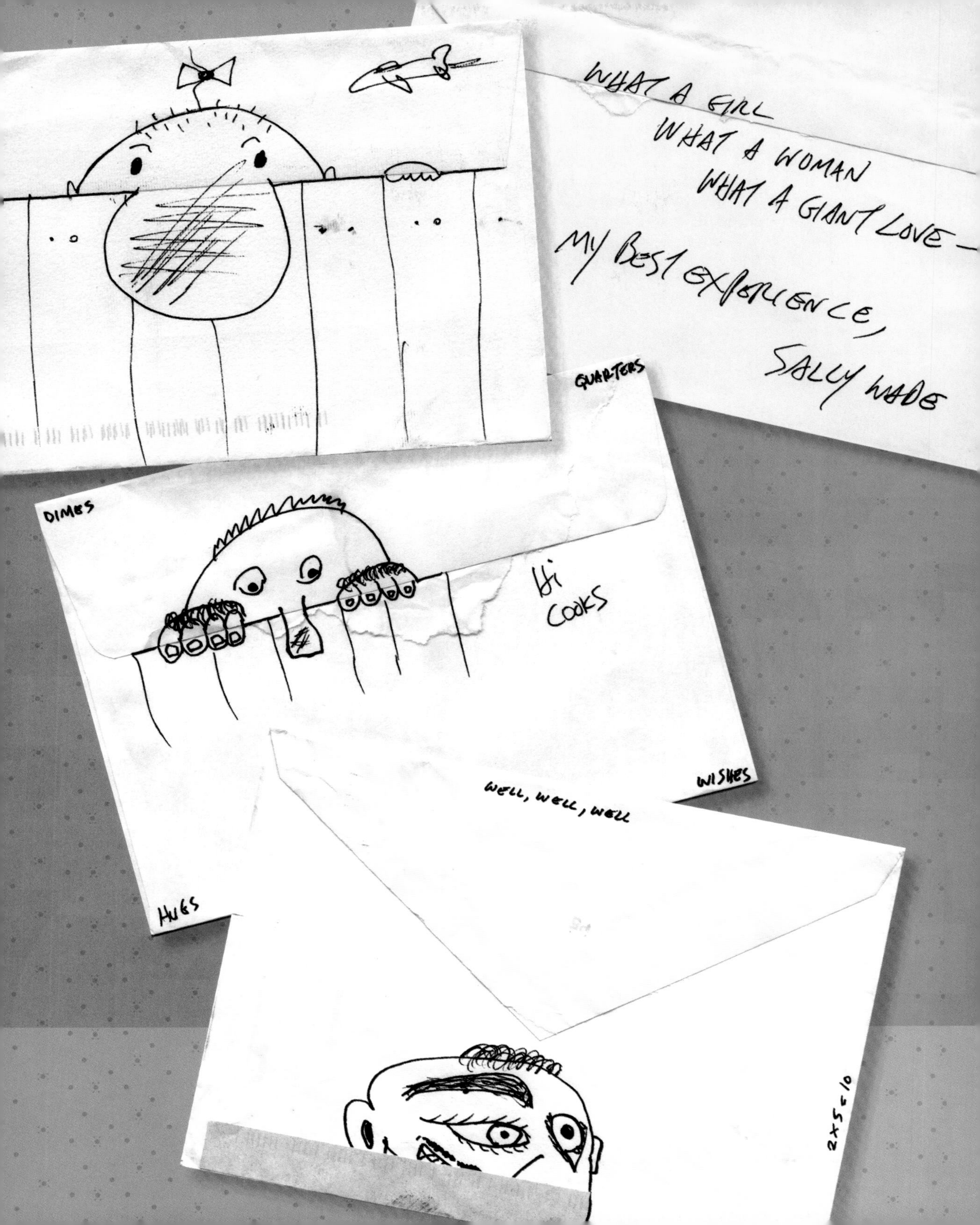

WHAT A GIRL
WHAT A WOMAN
WHAT A GIANT LOVE—

MY BEST EXPERIENCE,

SALLY WADE

QUARTERS

DIMES

Hi
COOKS

WISHES

WELL, WELL, WELL

HUGS

2x5-10

"HOOKIN' UP IN REAL TIME"

The couple flipped
as Jupiter dipped,
fifteen degrees an hour.

The moon rose
the couple froze,
bathed in heavenly power.

Hookin' up in real time;
workin' out our deal time;
lots of sex-appeal time;

By God, I think it's mealtime!

— The new poet

Sally
Sweetness

OUR LOVE

So much,

So sudden,

So powerful,

So like a dream ;

So deep,

So holy,

So mystical,

It can't be a dream.

You are (all things) light,
" " (" ") bright,
You are ALL THINGS pure and true

I AM (all things) ~~HERE~~ DEAR

I am (all things) ~~DEAR~~ DEAR

I AM (all things) ~~HERE~~ FOR YOU.

Your man,
George

SARAH

JANE

WITH THE GOLDEN MANE -
TOUCHES MY BODY
AND I GO INSANE.

MAY 99

SALLY WADE
COLLECTS TEN KISSES
from *George Carlin*

NEGOTIABLE ONLY BY MS. WADE

STUD MUFFIN,

HAVE A

GREAT TRIP

BABY- YOU ARE

MY HERO AND
MY INSPIRATION.
I LOVE YOU MADLY
BRIDGE BABIES FOREVER

YER
IN
MY
BRAIN.
DEEP!

GEORGE IS
LUCKY HE FOUND
SALLY.

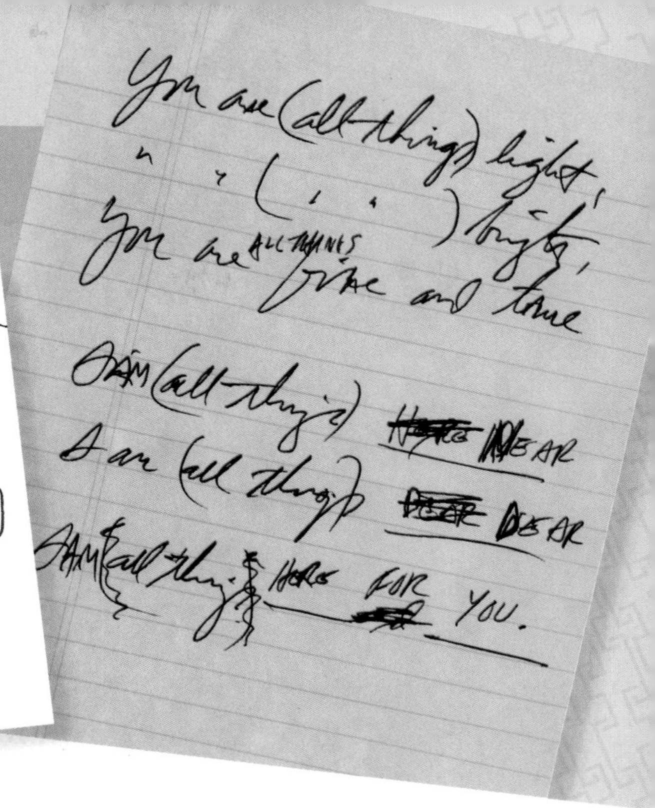
You are (all things) light,
" " (" ") bright,
You are ALL THINGS pure and true
I AM (all things) NEAR
I am (all things) DEAR
I AM (all things) HERE FOR YOU.

YOU
ME
HOW COME YOU SO FINE?

Geo's bush drawing

HEY LEETS!
IF YOU TOOK ALL DOGS THAT
EVER ~~BARKED~~ TIMES ALL THE
CHICKENS THAT EVER CLUCKED,
TIMES ALL THE PIGS THAT EVER
SQUEALED, TIMES ALL THE DUCKS
THAT EVER QUACKED —
AND MULTIPLIED THE TOTAL
BY ALL THE LITTLE GIRLS THAT
EVER GIGGLED OR CRIED,
OR SMILED OR SIGHED,
OF FELT A BIT SHY AND
TRIED TO HIDE;
YOU'D HAVE A VALUE EQUAL TO
A GRAIN OF THE LOVE-SAND ON THE BEACH
OF MY HEART — ALL FOR YOU.

Geo does the math again

Sal's cock tree

cock tree

بدر على التأجيل لتقديم... ان المهندس سيد م... ان من طلب...
ن على طلبى ... غسافرت —

Susan Jakobson ©1997

THE "NO-THEME" CARD ←

SALLUS!
THIS IS A GOOD CARD FOR
JUST SAYIN' HOW MUCH
I LOVE YA!
IF YOU TOOK ALL THE SWEET
THOUGHTS EVER THOUGHT BY
SARA JANE AND MULTIPLIED
THEM BY ALL THE SWEET SMILES
LITTLE GEO'GE EVER SMILED
BY LOOKIN' AT SARA JANE —
AND MULTIPLIED ALL THAT BY
THE NUMBER OF GRAINS OF SAND
IN THEIR SANDBOX — YOU'D KNOW
A TEENY BIT OF HOW MUCH I
LOVE YOU.   YORE GUY, GEORGE

NOTE #2 A
MORNING POEM
EXCELLENT DUMP,
FINE PEE!
GOOD WALK,
HIM + ME

Love + Smooches,
LONGFELLOW

KISSES ON THE BRIDGE

KISSES ON THE BRIDGE
PASTA IN THE ROOM
HONEY IN MY BED
BINGO! ZOWIE! BOOM!

(I DON'T DO FEET WELL)

I LOVE YOU MORE THAN ALL THE MARCHERS IN ALL OF HISTORY'S PARADES, TIMES ALL THE NOTES PLAYED BY ALL THE BANDS, TIMES ALL THE CORNS ON ALL THE FEET, TIMES ALL THE FROZEN FINGERS. AND THAT'S JUST A START. I'LL TELL YOU MORE TONIGHT. SEE YA THEN.

TO BEANIE BABY

YOU'RE MY BEANBAG BABY — I LOVE YOU MORE THAN ALL THE BEANS TIMES ALL THE BAGS, TIMES ALL THE DISTANCES BEAN BAGS EVER WERE THROWN, TIMES ALL THE PEOPLE WHO EVER RIPPED OPEN A BEAN BAG TO GET THE BEANS OUT, TIMES ALL THOSE BEANS THEY GOT OUT.

LOVE GEOGIE

Hey —   10/26

Sally sweetness
Sally silk
Sally of my dreams,

I ache my love,

altogether,

Dude,

Your person

Hey there, lovely —

Thanks for bein' a great pal, great partner, great lover and an exceptional vacation-taker.

I would have fun bein' with you even if we stayed a week in West Hell. I love you —
Travellin' Man

(EDITED)
You're every boy's dream

And every man's desire

(FINAL VERSION)

If you'll be my rose,

I'll be your sunflower.

GEOG

BOY OH BOY OH BOY OH BOY, DO
I MISS MY SWEET SALLY.
HER SMILE, HER TOUCH, HER
SWEET LIPS — HER WHOLE WONDER-
FUL SELF. SHE IS MY DREAM.

I love you with my
complete heart. Every cell
in my body vibrates with
your love. I am complete
because you have given
me your heart.
Be mine forever.
Your love, George

Sweetness,

Meet me in the
back yard

where Jupiter and the moon
play tag

and Sally and George
rule the day.

Anon.

MY
LUSCIOUS
LADY,

I'M BUGGY OVER YOU !

YOUR SWEET
LOVIN'
MAN

HEY, BUSY GIRL!

THIS IS →

A
MASSIVE
UNDERSTATEMENT.

IT'S MUCH DEEPER
THAN LOVE.

I love you

AND I THINK YOU'RE DOING
GREAT THINGS ON MANY LEVELS.

YOU RE-IMPRESS ME EVERY DAY.
JUST WHEN I THINK I KNOW YOUR
LIMITS, YOU SURPRISE ME.   LOVE
FROM YOUR GREATEST ADMIRER.

THERE ARE CLOUDS UNDER
HERE
AND ONE MORE BIRD ↓

Hey Sally — My Tea Bird

I just want to write one card like this — a card that ~~simply~~ tells you how much you mean to me.

There is not one small detail of my life that has not been turned upside-down and inside out by the presence of your love. It is all so positive and thrilling I can really find words for it. The sentences fall far short in et passing the depth of my

Passion, concern, interest care and love for you. You are ~~AT ONCE~~ my center and the other half of me. I never stop feeling good these days.

Thanks for that,

Love,

Yo Sleepin' Buddy,

Big Geogie

Hey! WOULD I WASTE A NICE BLANK SPACE A LIKE THIS ONE? F-U-U-U-CK NO! YOU REALLY SUMPN!

SNOW & GRAHAM
CHICAGO

LA →
← LV

LADY OF MY HEART —
    SALLY + GEORGE ARE SURPRISED
TO FIND THAT GAMBLING IS LEGAL
IN BELIZE. THEY PROMPTLY HIT
THE JACKPOT ON A MACHINE
THAT PROMISES ETERNAL LIFE.
THEY DECIDE TO SPEND THE TIME
IN BED. ~~~~ AT LEAST UNTIL
~~~~ TIME ENDS. SQUEEZE
                            A LITTLE
  IT NEVER ENDS.
P.S. THE ANDREWS SISTERS DROP IN.
YOURS UNTIL JUPITER RINGS,

CHAPTER 23

The Afterlife and Our
Current Communication

There are no regrets on my part. Everything was said. Everything was expressed. I just have a lot more to tell him. He left while our story was still in progress. That's why it's up to me to continue it. Just like I have to trust that someday we'll be together again, and as he promised, GEORGE CARLIN WILL FOREVER, PERMANENTLY COURT SALLY WADE.

Maybe

WE'LL LIVE
FOREVER —

TO MY ALL,

— AND MAYBE IT'LL
JUST
FEEL
LIKE
THAT.

YOUR ONE
GEORGE

To my Sally—

How sweet it would be
to have wings — and to
take flight with you. To
a place high up and far
away — where we could
live and love above the
clouds till the end of all
days.

Hey! Sounds like Jupiter.
And we don't need wings.
Just each other. C'mon,
let's take off.

THE ONE WHO ADORES GEORGE

AN ANGEL OF COOL

IN THE HOSPITAL, GEO MAKES A SPLIT-SECOND DECISION TO GO—AND THE JUPITER TWINS ABRUPTLY LET GO OUT OF LOVE. His brain is so quick that Sal is sure all other possibilities are revealing themselves to him at once. His soul and spirit somehow know it's the best time to go, and on some unconscious higher level, I agree. On a conscious lower level, I can only disagree, telling him to hang on, as he repeatedly says to me, "I'm sorry, babe." It was two days before our tenth anniversary. I lie beside him afterward and hold him, **thanking him for the best ten years of my life.**

EVERYTHING THAT IS OCCASIONALLY NUMBED WAS BROUGHT FRONT AND CENTER TODAY, AS I SAT DOWN TO WRITE THIS CHAPTER.
If I didn't believe that Geo's presence is with me now, I'd go with him in a New York minute. But I do.

WHAT GEO COMMUNICATES TO SAL AFTER HE CROSSES THE BRIDGE . . .
In fact, the first thing he said to me after he died is:

"JonBenét Ramsey's mother really did kill her."

"How do you know?" I ask. "Didn't she take a lie detector test?"

Geo: "Because the daughter is in heaven and I can't find the mother," he says. "So I put two and two together. Heaven and hell."

SAL: "The first thing you have to say to me after you die is that JonBenét Ramsey's mother really did kill her? Can't you think of something more important than that?"

GEO: "Well, Russia was never a threat. It was just made to seem that way. And a chemical put in gasoline to clean up the air is polluting the drinking water."

He communicates with me daily. Especially when I'm taking a shower. Not so much when I'm shopping at Whole Foods. I tell my therapist that as soon as I take my clothes off and get in the shower, there he is. I swear to God. "So he waits until you're vulnerable, right?" she asks. I say,

"No, he waits until I'm **n a k e d .**"

The other day I sensed him running around in my therapy session without his clothes on just to show me he still has a "body." I tell him he doesn't have to flash me, I'll take his word for it.

HE'S LEARNING TO HOVER, THEN SHOOT AWAY AND COME RIGHT BACK AGAIN

"Shooting away is the hard part," I can hear Geo say, "because you can get lost and misjudge where you're landing. Might be in a field somewhere in Kansas or a thornbush in Russia." Then *WHOOSH*, there he goes. Impressively, I might add. "Although he might have landed in the bushes again," Spot says. "Somewhere in Romania this time."

Hey Venus —

Jupiter is not our only heavenly benefactor. The Moon looks after us all the time — and is pleased with us as we ride the waves and propel the bubble upward. The look on his face says it all — he/she's never been happier. HAPPIER.

You're my sky and my star-field and my infinite heaven. Bless you Geze

now grab my balls

LOVE DRAWS HIM IN

So I say to him, **"Why not just stay here with me?"** And he communicates that it's because he's multitasking on several different levels. He can't get everything done if he's with me all the time. He says, "Stuff today, stuff tomorrow, and stuff next week all takes place at once because there's no time here, so I'm getting way behind on my to-do list. It's annoying."

"Oh," I say. "What's on your list besides loving me?"

"Planning our future," he says. "Ironing out all the details. Making sure you advance to my level with little effort—in fact, no effort at all. Jupiter Geo and Jupiter Sal will always be in the same place at the same time, sharing the same space in 'the bubble.'"

Things Geo has told me about **the afterlife** so far:

- There are a lot of people here who look alike. Especially twins and triplets.

- There's no booze unless you steal it from real people.

- We aren't the ones turning lights on and off the way most remaining family members think on Earth; that's because of an ongoing electrical storm on Mars.

- Nobody has to go to the bathroom so they've dispensed with toilet paper, pardon the pun.

- Private rooftop airports are popular for those who can't quite teleport yet.

- There's no money, so everybody has to beg "the source" for stuff, making house foreclosures common.

- I'm thinking of changing my favorite number from 58 to 162.

A few things Sal's told Geo about **this life so far:**

- My plan is to get up earlier, so I can give even more people trouble.

- I promised my inner child a bright, shiny new car if we stayed off Diet Coke for ninety days. Wait'll she finds out I lied.

- Without thinking, today I went into Starbucks wearing my pajamas. Then I forgot a straw, so I had to go back inside. When I tell Kelly (Geo's daughter), she figures no one was caffeinated enough to notice . . . "Unless you were wearing some slinky lingerie number. . . . You weren't, were you?"

- "I don't wanna scratch your butt! Go lie down!" Guess who I just said that to . . .

- Even though you weren't there to read to me, I did not scratch my forehead when it itched in the middle of the MRI!

- The other day I noticed my left ear looks different than my right ear. And I never knew that before.

- I meant to ask you, how do you know whether or not to tell someone they smell good when it might be their deodorant?

- Bursting into **tears** day.

HEY CRYBABY—

YOUR TEARS TASTE SWEETER THAN WINE. I WILL ALWAYS LICK THEM FROM YOUR FACE AND WIPE THEM FROM YOUR LIFE.

GEORGE

BALLY'S
LAS VEGAS
25th Anniversary

GEO STILL LOOKS OUT FOR SAL

Today he tells me to stay inside the protective bubble and to think of it whenever I can. He also says he'll be with me, and, at the same time, out doing other things. "That sound fair to you?" I ask. "All of me stuck here on Earth with parts of you flying around out there?" Then he says to turn and look at the card on my table and remember what it says . . .

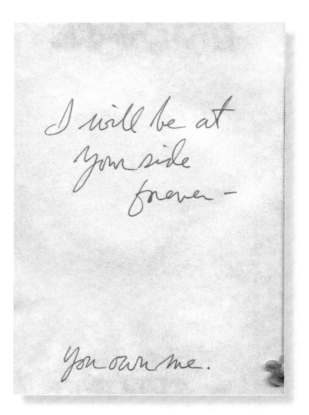

I will be at
your side
forever —

You own me.

"Okay, Geo," I say. "I'll remember that."

The Afterlife: Where one day, once again, Geo walks through the curtain, showing Sal her future.

Our real names are *Jupiter Geo* and *Jupiter Sal* and I swear this is all true. It's where we, the Jupiter twins, originated and where we will end up together again someday.

ALL THE ABOVE IS TRUE.

My Baby — ♡♡ COOKIES IS THE BEST

This card is pretty, but nothing is as pretty as you, my soul-mate and my eternal other/self.

Sweet love forever — George

JUST TWO —
TOGETHER
IN
BEAUTY

-SEE YOU ON THE BRIDGE

YOUR LOVER, GEORGE

When Sal gets home from the hospital, she opens Geo's computer and finds a file of all the music CDs he's ever made for her on his desktop along with these words:

I LOVE YOU EVEN MORE

I LOVE YOU EVEN MORE

I LOVE YOU EVEN MORE

I LOVE YOU EVEN

MORE

I LOVE YOU

EVEN MORE

I LOVE YOU

EVEN MORE

I LOVE YOU MORE THAN EVER!!

Along with this note propped in front of her computer

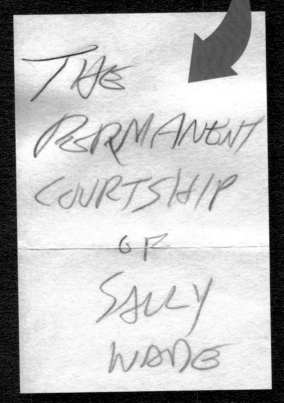

THE PERMANENT COURTSHIP OF SALLY WADE

BODY BABY
C/O THE END OF THE WORLD
RIGHT NEAR
JUPITER

HEY LUSCIOUS —

DONT BE SAD TOO
MUCH — I LOVE YOU,
AND I WANT TO
MAKE YOU THE HAPPIEST
WOMEN IN THE UNI-
VERSE. LET'S STAND
ON THIS BRIDGE AND
SING TO THE STARS OF
OUR LOVE

WED. NITE

Sally just called back
to say, "I love you. You're
the greatest thing in my
life." Wow — I'm so
fuckin' lucky!

Dearest Sally —
It's only Wednesday —
I haven't left yet, but
I miss you anyway.
Every day with you is
an absolutely wondrous
adventure. Our time to-
gether is so sweet and
so full of meaning. I
'm in awe of all this.
YOUR PERMANENT
LOVER —
Steve

I
LOVE
HER

Pearlie —

I believe in the rose called Sally —
I believe in the flower of our love.

I believe in the growth of our spirits and the development of our life together.

I believe you are the finest thing to ever appear in my life. I believe in you —
Love & Happy June 24

"It's believing in roses that makes them bloom."
♥ French proverb
Jerry

— SALLY —

— I LOVE YOU —

HANG IN AND FIGHT !!

GO FORWARD —

— I LOVE YOU —

— YOU'RE STRONG AND YOU CAN GET BACK ON TRACK —

YOU WILL —

HANG IN AND FIGHT

I LOVE YOU

THIS SOFT PIECE OF STEEL NAMED S.W.
— VELVET STEEL —

Hey, LUMINOUS!

We're about 35,000 feet closer to Jupiter than we were last night. and we're floating above the clouds ... again.

FUCK JOHN GLENN, WE ARE THE TRUE SPACE CADETS.

How I worship you— my stellar object. The only light in my sky. Shine on, Sally.

from YOUR
ORBITING
SATELLITE

S YOU
SHINE
LIKE
10,000,000,000
STARS.
AND YOU FILL
MY HEART

Geo and Sal's **future** plans

I BELIEVE THAT WE HAVE FAR MORE CHOICES IN OUR LIVES THAN OUR CURRENT REALITY SUGGESTS.
And I know that the decision to let Geo "go" was made by both of us—out of love—knowing it was the best decision at the time. I also know that Geo plans everything—every appointment, every nap, every performance was planned years in advance. He even planned meeting Sal. He told me he sat down and wrote a description of the kind of woman he'd like to meet after his wife of thirty-one years died—and then I walked into the bookstore.

I also know that he planned to die that day in the hospital. He carefully packed his suitcase for his exploratory surgery a week ahead of time, with deliberation and great care, leaving all the music he'd ever given me in a file called "Songs for Sally" open on his computer screen. I also know that right now he's making plans for the two of us and will be there to greet me when I step through that bright tunnel of light. In fact, he's coming almost all the way through to grab me so I don't get lost in transition.

And in the same way I trusted that he'd keep his promise to call me in four months when we first met, I know **I can still trust him now**—that he's planning our future together on **Jupiter.**

HEY COOKS —

WORK THE
JUMBLE

AND GIVE YOURSELF
A BIG HUG
IF YOU GET IT
RIGHT.

CAKE MAN

TO MY DESERT DREAM—
    YOU FLASH THROUGH MY MIND
AND HEART LIKE A WONDROUS
COMET — FULL OF LIFE AND
LIGHT ... AND LOVE.
    THE STARRY NIGHT IS NEVER
MORE BRIGHT AND MAGNIFICENT
THAN WHEN YOU'RE STANDING
OUTSIDE UNDER THE STARS.
    I MISS MY JUPITER
BUDDY — BUT SOON WE'LL
FROLIC UNDER JUPITER'S
BEAUTIFUL LIGHT.
                    LOVE TO YOU,
                    GEORGE

YOU KNOW WHEN
I KNEW YOU
REALLY
LOVED
ME?

"Shhh . . . the book's over, baby."

FUCK 'EM!
'EM!

love,
Mom

Acknowledgments

This book is dedicated to Sal's model guy, **Geo.**

First of all, I'd like to thank my agent, the amazing **Dan Strone**, who put me on my path and had the savvy and foresight to introduce me to my editor, the incredible **Trish Boczkowski**, who said I had a "beat-poet patois," and held my vision as well as my hand, and made the book sound better than I thought it could, then introduced me to her assistant, **Kate Dresser**, who worked harder than anyone, and with Trish, brought the story to art director **Jane Archer**, who worked her magic with visuals that bedazzled me, which led to the illustrious **Lyuba DiFalco**, Dan Strone's assistant, who did such a great job with the research that I'd marry her if we were gay, even though it still isn't legal in most states.

Special thanks also to other people who were also supportive and loved Geo very much, his daughter **Kelly Carlin**, and manager **Jerry Hamza**, my distinguished neighbor **Orson Bean** and his wife **Alley Mills** (who still thinks he introduced me to Geo, no matter what Spot says), my friend and writing mentor, **Jean Noel Bassior**, my guru and the facilitator of my inner-troll, **Jack Etlin**, and my brother, **Tom Wade** and his wife, **Lois**. I'd also mention my brother **Jim**, but I'll spare him the humiliation of having me as his little sister.

Spot's thanks go to **Starbucks**, **Petco**, and **Mr. Kim**'s corner store where he gets his liquor (the only three places that will let him inside.) Actually, Spot says Mr. Kim won't let him inside, but he's hoping he will if he mentions his store in these credits.

IMAGE CREDITS

168: photograph by author; 168: photograph by author; 169: photograph by author; 170: © Phillis Galembo 1982; 171: photograph by author; 171: photograph by author; 172: photograph by author; 172: © Michal Sowa, Berlin. www.inkognito.de; 172: photograph by author; 173: screenshot from *I Love Lucy* © CBS; 173: photograph by author; 174: photograph © GaryGoldbergphotograph.com; © Palm Press, 1998; 176: classicstock.com; 176: photograph by Hyla Molander; 178: photograph by author; 178: © Anne Geddes, courtesy Anne Geddes; 179: photograph © Gail Skoff; © Palm Press, Inc. 1996; 180: photograph © James Longo; Palm Press, Inc. 1995; 180: photograph © Suzanne Szasz; 181: photograph © Suzanne Szasz; 182: © Nouvelless Images; 184: 1961 Corbis; 185: photograph by author; 185: photograph by author; 185: photograph by author; 185: photograph by author; 186: H. Armstrong Roberts/Classicstock; 186: H. Armstrong Roberts/Classicstock; 187: H. Armstrong Roberts/Classicstock; 188: image from photo by Burns Flugum © 1983; 189: H. Armstrong Roberts/ Classicstock; 190: image from postcard © Santoro Graphics, Ltd. London; 194: photograph by author; 195: photograph by author; 197: photograph by author; 199: photograph by author; 200: photograph by author; 202: postcard © Fotofolio; 202: photograph by author; 203: image from photograph © Emil Schulthuss; 204: Nouvelles Images; 205: photograph by author; 205: image from postcard © Fotofolio; 206: photograph by author; 207: photograph by author; 208: photograph ©1998 Howard Berman; © Palm Press, Inc. 1998; 210: From Zolot of California collection (1952), courtesy Jean-Noel Bassior; 211: Meri Meri Inc.; 213: Nouvelles Images; 213: Nouvelles Images; 214: Nouvelles Images and Carles C. Ebbets; 215: photograph by author; 215: image from photograph © David Lombard; 216: photograph by author; 216: photograph by author; 216: photograph by author; 216: photograph by author; 217: photograph by author; 218: image from *The Amazing Colossal Man* © Orion Pictures; 222: Image via Kaleidescope; 223: Courtesy of Paper House Productions, Saugerties NY; 224: © Nouvelles Images and Michael Kenna; 225: photograph by author; 226: photograph by author; 227: photograph by author; 229: image from photograph © Eugene Smith; 230: photograph by author; 231: photograph by author; 232: image by Edward Hopper (1882–1967) *Nighthawks*; 233: photograph by author; 234: photograph by author; 235: photograph by author; 237: © Nouvelles Images and Stephanie Rausser; 237: © Nouvelles Images and Philippe Ughetto; 238: Getty Images; 239: photograph by author; 239: Getty Images; 240: Thinkstock.com; 243: photograph by author; 248: postcard © Fotofolio NY, NY, image © Elliott Erwitt/Magnum photographs, Inc.; 252: © Keith Baker; 254: photograph © Wayne Miller; © Palm Press, Inc. 1999; 255: photograph by author; 258: image from postcard © Photographic Images; 259: screenshot from *King Kong;* 261: photograph by author; 261: Art © Helena Nelson-Reed; 262: photograph by author; 281: image from greeting card © a Roger la Borde Design; 283: image from postcard © Fotofolio, photographer unidentified; 285: photograph by Peggy Sirota; 291: photograph by author; 295: photograph by author; 299: photograph by Peggy Sirota; custom surface designs of backgrounds by Jane Archer/ www.psbella.com.